Human Resource Development and Employee Relations

Pippa Riley

Viva Books

New Delhi | Mumbai | Chennai | Kolkata | Bengaluru | Hyderabad | Kochi | Guwahati

First Indian Edition 2011

VIVA BOOKS PRIVATE LIMITED

- 4737/23 Ansari Road, Daryaganj, New Delhi 110 002
  E-mail: vivadelhi@vivagroupindia.net, Tel. 42242200
- 76, Service Industries, Shirvane, Sector 1, Nerul, Navi Mumbai 400 706
  E-mail: vivamumbai@vivagroupindia.net, Tel. 27721273, 27721274
- Jamals Fazal Chambers, 26 Greams Road, Chennai 600 006
  E-mail: vivachennai@vivagroupindia.net, Tel. 28290304, 28294241
- B-103, Jindal Towers, 21/1A/3 Darga Road, Kolkata 700 017
  E-mail: vivakolkata@vivagroupindia.net, Tel. 22836381, 22816713
- 7, Sovereign Park Apartments, 56-58, K. R. Road, Basavanagudi, Bengaluru 560 004
  E-mail: vivabangalore@vivagroupindia.net, Tel. 26607409, 26607410
- 101-102 Mughal Marc Aptt., 3-4-637 to 641, Narayanguda, Hyderabad 500 029
  E-mail: vivahyderabad@vivagroupindia.net, Tel. 27564481, 27564482
- First Floor, Beevi Towers, SRM Road, Kaloor, Kochi 682 018, Kerala
  E-mail: vivakochi@vivagroupindia.net, Tel: 0484-2403055, 2403056
- 232, GNB Road, Beside UCO Bank, Silpukhuri, Guwahati 781 003
  E-mail: vivaguwahati@vivagroupindia.net, Tel: 0361-2666386

Published by arrangement with

BPP Learning Media Ltd.
BPP House, Aldine Place
London W12 8AA

ISBN : 978-81-309-1759-7

Published by Vinod Vasishtha for Viva Books Private Limited, 4737/23, Ansari Road, Daryaganj, New Delhi - 110 002.

Printed and bound by Raj Press, R-3, Inderpuri, New Delhi - 110 012.

Contents

Introduction

Viva-BPP Learning Media's Business Essentials range is the ideal learning solution for students studying for business-related qualifications and degrees. The range provides concise and comprehensive coverage of the key areas that are essential to the business student.

Qualifications in business are traditionally very demanding. Students therefore need learning resources which go straight to the core of the topics involved, and which build upon students' pre-existing knowledge and experience. The BPP Learning Media Business Essentials range has been designed to meet exactly that need.

Features include:

- In-depth coverage of essential topics within business-related subjects
- Plenty of activities, quizzes and topics for discussion to help retain the interest of students and ensure progress
- Up-to-date practical illustrations and case studies that really bring the material to life
- A full index, with key terms highlighted in bold

Each chapter contains:

- An introduction and a list of specific study objectives
- Summary diagrams and signposts to guide you through the chapter
- A chapter roundup, quick quiz with answers and answers to activities

Titles in the Series

- Accounts
- Business Decision Making
- Business Environment
- Business Maths
- Business Strategy
- Economics
- Finance: Management Accounting and Financial Reporting
- Human Resource Development and Employee Relations
- Human Resource Management
- Management: Communications and Achieving Results
- Management: Leading People and Professional Development
- Managing Finance
- Marketing and Promotion
- Marketing and Sales Strategy
- Marketing Principles
- Organisations and Behaviour
- Research Project

Study Guide

This Course Book includes features designed specifically to make learning effective and efficient.

- Each chapter begins with a summary diagram which maps out the areas covered by the chapter. There are detailed summary diagrams at the start of each main section of the chapter. You can use the diagrams during revision as a basis for your notes.
- After the main summary diagram there is an introduction, which sets the chapter in context. This is followed by learning objectives, which show you what you will learn as you work through the chapter.
- Throughout the Course Book, there are special aids to learning. These are indicated by symbols in the margin:

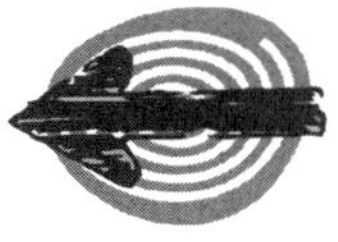

Signposts guide you through the book, showing how each section connects with the next.

Definitions give the meanings of key terms. The *glossary* at the end of the book summarises these.

Activities help you to test how much you have learned. An indication of the time you should take on each is given. Answers are given at the end of each chapter.

Topics for discussion are for use in seminars. They give you a chance to share your views with your fellow students. They allow you to highlight holes in your knowledge and to see how others understand concepts. If you have time, try 'teaching' someone the concepts you have learned in a session. This helps you to remember key points and answering their questions will consolidate your knowledge.

Examples relate what you have learned to the outside world. Try to think up your own examples as you work through the Course Book.

Chapter roundups present the key information from the chapter in a concise format. Useful for revision.

- At the end of each chapter, there is a **chapter roundup** and a **quick quiz** with answers. Use these to revise and consolidate your knowledge. The chapter roundup summarises the chapter. The quick quiz tests what you have learned (the answers often refer you back to the chapter so you can look over subjects again).

- At the end of the book, there is an index.

Part A

Human Resources Development

Chapter 1:

LEARNING AND THE LEARNING ORGANISATION

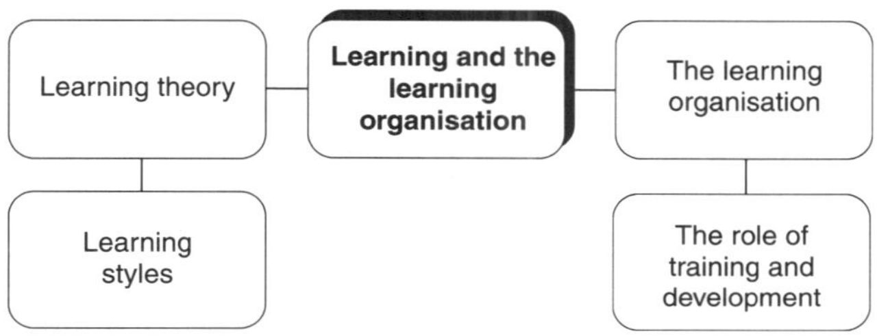

Introduction

Providing the organisation with the most suitable human resources for the task and environment is an on-going process. It involves not only recruitment and selection as discussed in the Human Resources Management Course Book, but the training and development of employees in order to help them meet current and potential future requirements.

In recent years, there has been a shift in emphasis from **training**, as a separate activity aimed at improving competence in a particular job area, to **learning**, as the process by which individuals develop competence in *any* area, in response to changing requirements. Teaching people how to learn – and supporting their learning at and through their work – enables the organisation to develop human resources more flexibly: by fostering continuous learning to meet changing capability requirements *and* by adapting to the learning preferences and opportunities of individuals.

In this chapter we examine how people learn, and how learning might be built into organisational culture and practice. In the next chapter, we explore the systematic planning, design, implementation and evaluation of training and development. In Chapter 3, we survey a range of government-led initiatives aimed at developing life-long learning skills in the UK.

Your objectives

In this chapter you will learn about the following.

(a) Learning theories
(b) Different learning styles
(c) The impact of the learning curve and transfer of learning
(d) Implications of learning theories and styles for planning learning events
(e) The learning organisation
(f) How training contributes to the achievement of business objectives
(g) The role of training and development policy within the organisation

1 LEARNING THEORY

1.1 Three theoretical approaches

It is not possible to put forward a simple definition of learning, because despite intensive scientific and practical work on the subject, there are different ways of understanding how the process works, what it involves, and what we mean when we say that a person 'knows' something (epistemology).

There are three basic theories of how learning works.

(a) **The behaviourist (or stimulus-response) approach.** Behaviourist psychology is based on 'empirical' epistemology (the belief that the human mind operates purely on information gained from the senses by experience) and concentrates on observable behaviour, since 'thought processes' are not amenable to scientific study. It therefore concentrates on the relationship between stimuli (input through the senses) and the organism's responses to those stimuli. The work of Pavlov (on dogs) and Skinner (on rats) suggested that learning is the formation of new connections between stimulus and response on the basis of experience, which they called **conditioning.** According to this theory, we modify our responses to a given stimulus according to whether the feedback on the results of our previous responses was good or bad: an incentive (positive reinforcement) or deterrent (negative reinforcement) to similar behaviour in future. Repetition of the stimulus-response sequence strengthens the conditioning, making us more likely to respond in the same way in future.

(b) **The cognitive (or information-processing) approach.** Cognitive psychology is based on 'rationalist' epistemology (the belief that the human mind imposes organisation and meaning on sensory raw material) and assumes that it is possible to make inferences about those thought processes. According to this theory, our behaviour is 'purposive': we make plans of action in pursuit of goals that we value. Learning is the way in which we process and interpret feedback on the results of past behaviour/experience, and make decisions about whether to maintain successful behaviours or modify unsuccessful behaviours in future, in pursuit of our goals. We do not simply learn new habits (as conditioning theories suggest) but ways of dealing with information and choosing alternative methods of reaching our goals: we learn to learn.

(c) **The social learning approach.** Studies of child development suggest that human beings are designed to learn by imitating other people who are significant to us: our behavioural and role models (who shift over time from our parents and caregivers in childhood, to peers in adolescence, to selected experts and mentors in adulthood). We define our social identity and behaviour by reflection from other people: how they respond to us. We learn to perform actions by 'modelling': watching and analysing the way others do them, and imitating the successful aspects of their performance.

Activity 1 **(10 minutes)**

Before reading on, pick out the aspects of the theoretical approaches outlined above which might be important for the design of training programmes. (Think about your experiences of training/learning techniques, as you read about each theory...)

Implications for training design

Whichever approach it is based on, learning theory offers certain useful propositions for the design of effective training programmes.

(a) The individual should be **motivated** to learn. The purpose and benefits of a learning activity should be made clear, according to the individual's motives or goals: reward, challenge, competence or whatever. Organisational support is critical to the effectiveness of its members' learning.

(b) Clear **goals and objectives** should be set, so that each task has some meaning. This will help trainees in the control process that leads to learning, providing targets against which performance will constantly be measured and adjusted. Motivation to learn will be enhanced if the individual has been involved in setting his or her own learning goals.

(c) Learning should be **structured** and **paced** to allow learning processes to take place effectively and progressively. Each stage of learning should present a challenge (motivation), without overloading trainees so that they lose confidence and the ability to assimilate information/experience.

(d) **Exposure to learning materials** and interactive input (from learning software and/or from coaches or facilitators) enriches the cognitive process and encourages the internalisation of learning. Case studies, problem solving exercises and so on engage the purposive process of learning. Coaching, mentoring and team learning activities engage social learning.

(e) There should be timely, relevant **feedback** on performance and progress. This will usually be provided by the facilitator, and should be concurrent – or not long delayed. If progress reports or appraisals are given only at the course end, for example, there will be no opportunity for progressive behavioural adjustment.

(f) Positive and negative **reinforcement** should be judiciously used. Recognition and encouragement embeds correct learning and motivates further effort. Constructive criticism of errors is essential for learning, but must be used sensitively: 'punishing' error or slow progress may simply discourage the learner and create a culture of failure. (Even behaviourism notes that negative reinforcement merely conditions people to avoid error and punishment – not to find more constructive behaviours.) 'Failure' should be redefined as 'opportunity for learning'.

(g) Active **participation** in the learning experience (for example, in action learning or discovery learning) is generally more effective than passive reception (for example, in lectures or reading), because it enhances concentration and conditioning. Practice and repetition can be used to reinforce passive learning, but participation has the added effect of encouraging 'ownership' of the goals and process of change.

1.2 Stages of learning

The 'stages of learning' comprise a simple, intuitive model of the evolution of learned behaviour.

Stage 1. **Unconscious incompetence**. You aren't aware of what you don't know: you simply act in the way that seems best with the knowledge you have at the time.

Stage 2. **Conscious incompetence**. You become aware that you don't know. New information, feedback from others, or the results of your behaviour, suggest that there is something missing.

Stage 3. **Conscious competence**. You work at knowing. You research, analyse, practise, repeat, monitor, adjust. You may be competent – but it requires conscious thought and application.

Stage 4. **Unconscious competence**. You don't have to think about knowing. You have internalised the knowledge or skill and use it without having to think about it.

Think about the way a baby learns to walk, for example, and you will find that it corresponds to these four stages. The same goes for learning to type or to drive a car (remember how laborious the 'conscious competence' stage seemed?).

Activity 2 **(15 minutes)**

Illustrate the Stages of Learning with another example of learning a work-related skill.

1.3 The learning curve

Definition

A **learning curve** is a graph showing the relationship between the time spent in learning and the level of competence attained. Hence, it describes the progress and variable pace of learning. (It is common for people to say that they are 'on a steep learning curve' when they have to acquire a lot of new knowledge or skills in a short period of time.)

(Note that when used in this way, the phrase 'learning curve' means something different from its use in management science, where it means a mathematical function that describes the effect of experience in reducing cumulative manufacturing times.)

A learning curve may be used:

(a) To suggest **typical patterns** in the acquisition of a given skill or type of skill: the pace of skill acquisition, the standard at which performance 'levels out' (does not improve further); the point at which performance 'plateaus' (levels out for a while and then improves further).

(b) To illustrate the **progress of a given trainee's learning**/proficiency during the training process, in order to monitor the progress and pace of training – and to make allowances for different rates of learning and the 'steepness' of the curve where necessary.

(c) To **plan** the size of the 'chunks' to be taught in one session or stage of learning, the length of practice/consolidation periods before moving to the next stage and so on.

A 'standard' learning curve is initially steep, levelling out towards proficiency. However, in practice this will depend on the design of the learning programme (allowing for consolidation periods) and the motivation and aptitude of the learner. The curve for the acquisition of skills typically shows one or more plateaus, reflecting the trainee's need to consolidate what (s)he has learned so far, to correct some aspects of performance, to regain motivation and focus after the initial effort, or to establish habitual or unconscious competence in one skill prior to moving on to a new area. Momentum then gathers again, until the trainee reaches proficiency level, where the curve will level off – unless there is an injection of new equipment or methods, or fresh motivation, to lift output again. Such a learning curve is illustrated in Figure 1.1.

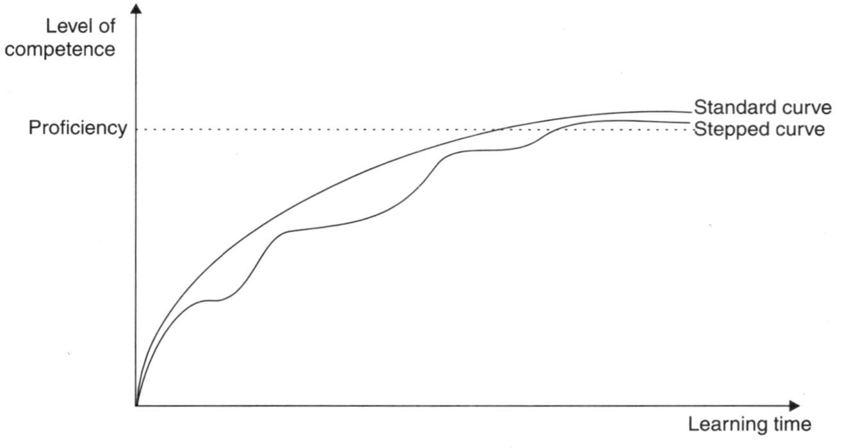

Figure 1.1: Learning curve

Note that learning curves can be quite complex, going down as well as up: for example, if the trainee is unable to practise or apply newly acquired skills and forgets them, or refuses to accept new areas of conscious incompetence which emerge in the course of training. An up-and-down '**transition curve**' is common in cases where an individual changes jobs or work methods, or makes the transition from a non-managerial to a managerial position.

Activity 3 **(20 minutes)**

Draw a learning curve for:

(a) An easy task that takes two weeks to learn.

(b) A complex task that takes eight weeks to learn, but for which the training programme has been 'paced' to include consolidation and problem-solving time.

You may have noticed that the stages of learning and the learning curve appear to be linear or progressive, but in fact form part of an on-going cycle or control system: discovering further areas of conscious incompetence, starting further learning curves in order to adjust performance in response to feedback. This aspect of learning has been formulated as 'the learning cycle'.

1.4 The learning cycle

The best known model is the **experiential learning cycle** devised by David Kolb (1984) and popularised by Honey and Mumford (1992). Kolb suggested that effective learning could start from concrete experience, as well as from abstract concepts. It should not be 'a special activity cut off from the real world and unrelated to one's life', but should integrate concrete (involvement) and abstract (detachment), active (doing) and reflective (observing) elements. This could be conceived as a simple cyclical process, as follows: Figure 1.2.

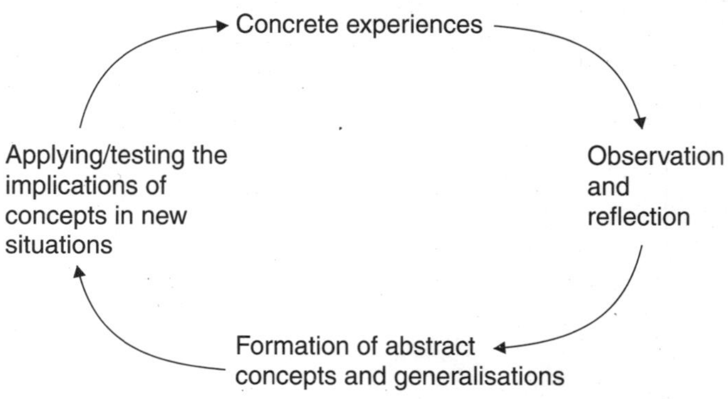

Figure 1.2: Experiential learning cycle

- **Having an experience**: being fully involved in an action or interaction, utilising your current knowledge and skills.
- **Reviewing the experience**: looking back at what happened, describing it, reflecting on the causes and effects of your behaviour.
- **Concluding from the experience**: forming generalisations, concepts and theories that will enable you to integrate your observations and reflections into your behaviour on future occasions or in other contexts.
- **Planning the next steps**: planning ways in which you can apply and test your conclusions in further action.

Suppose that an employee interviews a customer for the first time (*concrete experience*). He observes his own performance and the dynamics of the situation (*observation*). Afterwards, having failed to convince the customer to buy the product, he analyses what he did right and wrong (*reflection*). He comes to the conclusion that he failed to listen to what the customer really wanted and feared, underneath her general reluctance: he thinks that the key to more effective persuasion may be active listening (*abstraction/generalisation*). He decides to apply active listening techniques in his next interview (*application/testing*). This provides him with a new experience with which to start the cycle over again.

FOR DISCUSSION

Can you trace the phases of the learning cycle in the way your studies are structured? What phases are well provided for – and which might you require more opportunity for? Do some phases(s) of the cycle naturally appeal to you more than others?

Kolb recognised that people tend to have a preference for a particular phase of the cycle, which he identified as a preferred 'learning style'. We will discuss this aspect of learning theory in Section 2 of this chapter. Meanwhile, we will look at another issue raised by the experiential learning cycle: what is the relationship between theory and practice in learning? If you have read a book on how a car works, should you be able to drive it? If you can drive a car, do you need to be able to explain how it works? And if you have grasped both theory and practice of driving a car, should you also be able to drive a truck? The idea that we can learn something in one context and 'carry it across' to another context is called the **transfer of learning**.

1.5 Transfer of learning

Definition

> **Transfer of learning** refers to the extent to which newly learned information or skills have been transferred from the learning context to the application of a specific task.

Positive transfer refers to a situation in which learning has been successfully transferred to a task: negative transfer refers to a situation in which learning has not been transferred to the application of a task.

There are two basic approaches to the transfer of learning.

(a) **Transfer by specific correspondence of elements.**

If you were learning French, for example, you might listen to language tapes which feature the repetition and rehearsal of common phrases used in specific contexts: this would facilitate transfer of learning (use of these phrases) when you found yourself in those specific contexts. The workplace equivalent might be hands-on training in a specific administrative or technical procedure used by your employer.

The advantage of this approach, when the correspondences are strong, is that learning can be swiftly and effectively applied in the work context, where it will be further embedded and adapted. The danger with this approach is that if the context, procedure or equipment are not quite the same as the models used in your learning, you might not be able to 'generalise' in order to transfer learning to the new situation. Indeed, the attempt to transfer learning may have a detrimental effect on its application, if the techniques learned in one context are actively 'wrong' in another and have to be unlearned.

(b) **Transfer by principle.**

Using the example of learning French again: you might use a method which went through the grammatical rules of the language. This might facilitate transfer of learning to a range of situations, since you could simply slot in specific contextual vocabulary as you acquired it. The workplace equivalent would be training which covered:

(i) The desired outcomes of performing a procedure (why it is performed)

(ii) Under what conditions this procedure is likely to be the most appropriate strategy among available alternatives

(iii) How to perform the procedure

(iv) How the stages of the procedure follow and depend on one another and what other variables influence performance

(v) Possible problems during a procedure and how to 'troubleshoot'

(vi) Sources of information and help, should they be required

The advantage of this approach is that it generalises learning and facilitates its transfer across a wider range of contexts. The danger, however, is that it may be too generalised to allow immediate application to a particular work context, and the knowledge may be forgotten if it is not immediately applied.

There is no right or wrong approach to transfer of learning. The nature of the task and the uniqueness or otherwise of the organisation's systems and 'house style' may dictate one or the other. In addition, some people have a preference for learning exactly what they need to do, by doing it: others prefer to work through a conceptual framework and then to apply what they know to a specific context. ('Learning styles' again: we will discuss them below.)

Whichever approach is used, organisations must take into account the transferability of learning if they are not to waste their training efforts and budgets. The range of contexts and variables, and the preferences of trainees, should be taken into account in designing training programmes where possible, to ensure positive transfer. Modern approaches to training (such as competence definition, employability training and attitude and awareness training) are designed to be widely transferable within the organisational context and in the personal lives of trainees.

In addition, practical measures are required to support transfer of learning. The worksite and job context are important in enabling trainees to apply newly-learned skills. They require:

- Appropriate **systems, tools and resources** to be available to apply their learning on the job, and
- Support from **supervisors, peers and co-workers** (if whole-team learning has not been used).

Activity 4 **(30 minutes)**

We have already mentioned some situations in which the learning curve levels out or even goes downwards: loss of motivation and negative transfer, for example. Can you think of other factors that might hinder or block learning? (Consider your work or study situation. What factors – cultural, emotional, intellectual, motivational, situational, physical – make it more difficult for you to learn than it needs to be?)

1.6 Whole or part learning

Learning may be done in whole or in part. Whole learning occurs where tasks are taught or modelled in their entirety. In part learning, tasks are broken down and taught and practised stage by stage, building up to the complete task.

The various theories we have discussed so far encourage a contingency approach to learning: the appropriate strategy and techniques will depend on (among other things) the preferences of the individual for active or reflective, concrete or abstract learning experiences. Several theorists have classified these preferences as distinct 'learning styles': we will discuss them now.

2 LEARNING STYLES

2.1 Honey and Mumford

Kolb (1984) recognised that people tend to have a preference for a particular phase of the experiential learning cycle, which he identified as a preferred **learning style**.

Honey and Mumford (1992) also noted that 'people vary not just in their learning skills but also in their learning styles. Why otherwise might two people, matched for age, intelligence and need, exposed to the *same* learning opportunity, react so differently?' Honey and Mumford formulated a popular classification of learning styles in terms of the attitudes and behaviours which determine an individual's preferred way of learning.

Style	Characteristics	Learning preferences
ACTIVIST *'I'll try anything once'*	Activists involve themselves fully in new experiences. They are open-minded and enthusiastic about new things – but easily bored by long-term implementation and consolidation: act first and think about consequences later. They prefer to tackle problems by brainstorming. They easily get involved with others – but tend to centre activities on themselves.	Learn best from activities which: • present new experiences/ problems • involve short 'here and now' activities • offer excitement, drama and variety • have high visibility/ limelight • allow them to generate ideas without constraints of structure or feasibility • challenge/throw them in at the deep end • involve them with other people • allow them to 'have a go'
REFLECTOR *'Look before you leap'*	Reflectors like to stand back to observe and ponder new experiences, preferring to consider all angles and implications, and to analyse all available data, before reaching any conclusions or making any moves. When they do act, it is from awareness of the big picture. They tend to adopt a low profile, taking a back seat in meetings and discussions – though listening and observing others carefully – and tend to have a slightly distant, tolerant, unruffled air.	Learn best from activities which: • encourage observation and reflection • allow them to stand back from events • allow them to think before acting • involve painstaking research • offer an opportunity for review • help them to exchange views with others without risk, with structure • allow them to arrive in their own time

Style	Characteristics	Learning preferences
THEORIST *'If it's logical it's good'*	Theorists are keen on basic assumptions, principles, theories, models and systems thinking. They are detached and analytical and like to analyse and synthesise facts and observations into coherent theories. They think problems through systematically and logically. They are interested in maximising certainty, and so tend to be rigidly perfectionist and uncomfortable with subjectivity, ambiguity, lateral thinking and flippancy.	Learn best from activities which: • relate to a system, model or theory • allow time to grasp underlying logic • display rationality or logic • have clear purpose and structure • allow analysis/generalisation of reasons for success/failure • stretch them intellectually
PRAGMATIST *'If it works, it's good* *(but there is always a better way)'*	Reflectors are eager to try out ideas, theories and techniques to see if they work in practice. They like to get on with things, acting quickly and confidently on ideas that attract them – and tending to be impatient with ruminating and open-ended discussion. They are down to earth: enjoying practical decisions and responding to problems and opportunities 'as a challenge'.	Learn best from activities which: • relate to work problems/ opportunities • offer techniques with obvious practical applications/advantages • allow practise with coaching/feedback from a credible expert • expose them to role models to imitate • allows them to concentrate on practical issues (plans, tips etc) • are followed up with immediate opportunities to implement learning

Source: compiled from Honey and Mumford (1992)

Training should ideally be designed to accommodate the preferences of all four styles. This can often be overlooked, especially as the majority of training staff are activists!

Activity 5 **(15 minutes)**

John, Paula, Ringo and Georgette are learning French, as part of their firm's initiative to develop staff in European markets.

(a) John reckons that since he does not actually speak to clients, the whole scheme is a waste of time. He claims to be too busy to attend classes.

(b) Paula loves the classes, because they simulate real conversational situations. The trainees have to use whatever vocabulary they have to get their meaning across, guided and corrected by the tutor. Paula doesn't like learning grammatical rules: she's happy to pick up the phrases to fit the situations.

(c) Ringo doesn't mind the teaching method either. He doesn't say anything for the first few minutes, though, just picks up what he can, gets it straight (allowing Paula to make the mistakes) and then comes out with a fluent response.

(d) Georgette is lost. She feels frustrated because, although she has learned the phrases for a given situation, she is not sure it will apply in other contexts. She takes home a book of grammar at night, to bone up on the general principles and rules.

Who represents which learning style? What style has the course been designed for?

2.2 Kolb's Learning Styles Inventory

Kolb's Learning Styles Inventory is designed to identify the preferences of learners for particular phases of the experiential learning cycle (see Paragraph 1.4 above).

For copyright reasons, the inventory cannot be reproduced here, but the broad categories of preference identified by Kolb are as follows.

(a) The '**converger**' (Abstracting/Generalising and Applying/Testing) prefers applying abstract generalisations in practical and specific ways.

(b) The '**diverger**' (Concrete Experience and Reflective Observation) prefers to reflect 'laterally' on specific experience from different points of view.

(c) The '**assimilator**' (Abstracting/Generalising and Reflective Observation) is comfortable with concepts and abstract ideas.

(d) The '**accommodator**' (Concrete Experience and Applying/Testing) prefers to learn primarily from doing.

2.3 The Myers-Briggs Type Indicator

The Myers-Briggs Type Indicator (MBTI) is a proprietary psychometric assessment of personality based on Jung's theory of psychological type. The test classifies people into sixteen carefully described types based on four dichotomies of characteristics.

(a) **Extraversion/introversion**: a preference for the external environment of behaviour and people or the internal environment of concepts and thinking

(b) **Sensing/intuition**: a preference for conscious or unconscious perception of the world

(c) **Thinking/feeling**: a preference for logic and reason or for internal processes including emotional reactions

(d) **Judgement/perception**: a preference for decision-making using thinking and feeling or sensing and intuition

The MBTI is widely used, though its utility for purposes of selection and career development is disputed. There seems to be little if any correlation between indicated type and suitability for any particular role.

Now that we have surveyed some of the theoretical framework of training, let's move on to its organisational framework.

3 THE ROLE OF TRAINING AND DEVELOPMENT

3.1 Outcomes of training and development

We have talked about learning in terms of acquiring the knowledge or ability to do something. In fact, training and development activities may be directed towards a number of different outcomes.

Skill

Definition

> **Skill** may be defined as a learned pattern of operations, or responses to stimuli, which allow the successful, rapid and apparently confident performance of a complex task.

Manual work is often divided into categories according to varying degrees of perceptual-motor skill required: 'skilled' (like electricians and vehicle mechanics), 'semi-skilled' (like machine operators) and 'unskilled' (like road sweepers and canteen assistants). The degree of skill attributed to these jobs is clearly associated with:

(a) The amount of learning required to master the necessary actions, techniques and methods

(b) The sophistication of perception and response required (eg diagnosing a fault and repairing a machine is more skilled work than simply operating it in accordance with learned methods).

Non-manual work involves a wide range of what are classified as 'higher order' thinking skills: cognitive (including information-processing and decision-making), creative, perceptual, linguistic/expressive, social/interpersonal and so on.

Knowledge

Knowledge is a very complex concept, but in the training context may be divided into two areas which are sometimes referred to as 'know-that' and 'know-how'.

(a) **'Know-that'** is knowledge *about* something or 'propositional knowledge': awareness of ideas, concepts, theories, methodologies and so on.

(b) **'Know-how'** is knowledge *of* something, or the ability to do something: 'practical knowledge'. This may be based on underlying, unverbalised, untaught knowledge ('tacit knowledge'), but is typically acquired through imitation and experience.

Propositional knowledge is commonly associated with formal education, and has traditionally attracted high status in the social hierarchy of skills – while at the same time attracting the suspicion of those with practical knowledge, who see it as divorced from real-world competence. At the end of this course, you may know how HRM 'should' be done – but actually doing it in an organisational setting may be something else again! An organisation clearly needs to acquire and develop both propositional knowledge (understanding of management and technical processes) and practical knowledge (ability to make those processes work in practice).

FOR DISCUSSION

Which is more useful to an organisation: 'know-that' (propositional knowledge) or 'know-how?' (practical knowledge)? Do you agree that 'those who can, do: those who can't, teach'?

Competence

Definition

> **Competence** may be defined as the skill, knowledge and behaviours that need to be applied for effective performance in a work context.

Competence represents one of the 'bundles' of practice which may contribute to the 'fit' or integration of HRM policies in an organisation. This is discussed in detail in the Human Resources Management Course Book. Competence frameworks may be used in HR planning, recruitment and selection, performance management, reward and training and development. There are two key elements in the concept.

(a) It integrates knowledge, skills and other attributes into the notion of overall ability.

(b) It defines and assesses ability in the context of workplace performance and proficiency.

Competency definition and testing have become a major element in the design of training and development in the UK: we will return to this theme in Chapter 3, where we trace the history of the competence movement.

Attitudes and awareness

Another recently-recognised area of training is aimed at encouraging trainees to gain insight into their own behaviour and to try to change the negative or restricting attitudes that prevent the individual from attaining more effective performance. Examples of training outcomes include:

(a) Assertiveness (a communication style which asserts one's rights, wishes and opinions in a straightforward, non-passive, yet non-aggressive manner which also respects the rights, wishes and opinions of others)

(b) Insight into the style and effectiveness of interpersonal relations and group dynamics (eg through encounter or 'T' groups)

(c) Insight into the motives underlying undesirable attitudes (racism, sexism, sexual harassment, bullying and so on)

(d) Self-awareness, social awareness, social skills and the ability to manage one's emotional responses (collectively called 'emotional intelligence').

Activity 6 **(10 minutes)**

Who do you think would benefit most from assertiveness training, and for what purpose?

Employability

Definition

Employability describes a portfolio of knowledge, skills, competences and attributes that enhances an individual's mobility and power in the labour market. Employability training aims to equip employees with such a portfolio.

Traditionally, training has been seen as a way of improving an employee's performance in a particular job or career path, for the benefit of the employing organisation. However, many organisations are no longer in a position to offer long-term job security to their employees. Socially responsible employers wish to clarify this new psychological contract and facilitate employees' transition to other jobs, by enhancing their employability portfolio – while simultaneously benefiting from the creation of a more flexible multi-skilled labour force.

What benefits can the organisation expect to gain from achieving the above outcomes? This is the first question in evaluating the role of training and development in the organisation.

3.2 Benefits of training and development activity

In so far as training and development activity (or a broader perception of learning) increases competency, skills, versatility, confidence, awareness, knowledge and further learning among employees, it may contribute to the business objectives of the organisation in a number of ways.

(a) Increased efficiency and productivity, through faster, more skilled work and greater labour flexibility (eg through multi-skilling)

(b) Reduction in costs, associated with the above, and with less wastage and fewer errors

(c) Reduction in interpersonal and performance-related problems – both because of enhanced competence and greater confidence

(d) Improved quality of work/service

(e) Fewer accidents and problems with equipment and machinery

(f) Enhanced ability to attract and retain high calibre employees

(g) Improved job satisfaction, motivation and morale among developed employees since skill and career development are key intrinsic rewards which may further increase productivity and quality

(h) Greater communication between employees on job-related issues, with potential for quality improvements and innovations

(i) Greater potential for increased empowerment and involvement of employees, as they become more aware and more skilled (particularly if training goes beyond technical skills to embrace communication and interpersonal skills, delegation skills for managers, problem-solving and decision-making skills and so on)

(j) The fostering of a culture of continuous learning and improvement, which promotes adaptability to change, organisational flexibility and a positive organisation culture

(k) Compliance with legislation and regulation (where training is given in health and safety measures, non-discrimination and so on)

(l) Better promotion and management succession planning, as employee potential is systematically developed

(m) Fulfilling the future needs of the organisation for skills which may be subject to shortages or fluctuations in the external labour market

(n) Corporate social responsibility (and enhanced employer/recruiter brand) through developing employees – particularly in general employability.

We will look at ways in which training and development activities can be evaluated (and justified in terms of their return on investment) in Chapter 2.

EXAMPLE: MOTOROLA

Motorola found itself trying to compete globally in a market of new technologies and changing demands, with people who, in many cases, had difficulty with reading and basic mathematics. It launched a wide-ranging scheme of education and training (its own 'University') for its employees – and for the employees of suppliers and key customers. Training was designed to develop the person, not just the company and the job. It was aimed at 'creating an environment for learning, a continuous openness to new ideas... We not only teach skills, we try to breathe the very spirit of creativity and flexibility into manufacturing and management.'

Activity 7 **(20 minutes)**

What might be the benefits of training to the trainee? (Think what you are getting out of doing this course, for example.)

List at least five benefits.

You might by now be thinking that training is obviously such a Good Thing that an organisation could not go wrong by simply 'providing some'. If performance is poor: do some training! If morale is low: do some training! If empowerment is a foreign concept in your organisation: do some training! Let's get things into perspective ...

Realistic expectations

The HR function must recognise – and emphasise to line managers – that:

(a) Training and development can improve performance
but

(b) There are many variables in job performance, not all of which may be addressed by training alone
and

(c) Even in areas susceptible to training, the training programme must be designed and implemented appropriately for the needs of the organisation and the specific group of trainees – or it will not be effective.

3.3 Stakeholders in human resource development

It is worth noting that there are a number of different stakeholders in organisational training and development. (Stakeholders are individuals or groups who have an interest or 'stake' in a given endeavour, because they have contributed to it and/or because they are affected by its outcomes.)

Potential stakeholders in training (in general, or particular training events) include:

(a) The owners and senior mangers of the organisation, who invest in human resource development and determine training policy to reap certain returns on their investment

(b) The line managers of trainees, whose units' performance will be affected by (positive or negative) changes in trainees' competence, behaviour and attitudes

(c) The trainees, who invest time, effort and a range of psychological resources in learning and whose competence, employability and job satisfaction are affected by the organisation's development policies (or lack of them)

(d) The training managers (planners, funders, providers, evaluators) who must develop and deliver successful training in order to meet their own objectives

(e) The instructors, coaches and mentors within the work team, who likewise measure their success by the effectiveness of the learning they deliver and support

(f) Training vendors (course providers, materials publishers, software developers, consultants) whose continued relationship with the firm, and business success, depends on positive evaluation by training managers and trainees

(g) The training community in general, whose reputation, viability and methodology depends on the standard and effectiveness of members' offerings and feedback from customers.

The design, planning, delivery and evaluation of learning and training events must take the needs, requirements, preferences and priorities of some or all of these stakeholders into account. As we will see in Chapter 2, most models of training evaluation recognise stakeholder experience and feedback (from at least some constituent groups) as an important measure of success.

FOR DISCUSSION

What do you think are likely to be the key evaluation criteria of each of the stakeholder groups listed above, in measuring the 'success' of a training event or programme? What might be the implications if each of these stakeholder groups were dissatisfied with the experience or outcomes of training?

3.4 The role of training and development policy

Armstrong (2009) suggests that:

> The objective of an organisation's policies, processes and programmes for the delivery of learning and training is to achieve its human resource development strategies by ensuring that it has the skilled, knowledgeable and competent people required to meet its present and future needs.

A human resource development policy will therefore address the following issues.

(a) Why does the organisation train and develop people: how is human resource development envisaged as contributing to strategic objectives and the HR plan? How does investment in it benefit organisational stakeholders?

(b) What are the desired outcomes of HRD: skills, knowledge, competence, awareness/attitudes, employability? How do these support business and other HRM strategies?

(c) How will learning and development needs and objectives be determined? How will they relate to individual, team and organisational performance and bottom-line results? What value is placed on employability and 'personal' development?

(d) Whom does the organisation intend to train and develop? What grades of employee will have access to training, of what type and at what level? What equal opportunity commitments should be made? (This may be part of a wider commitment to encouraging and supporting all members of the organisation to pursue continuous learning opportunities.)

(e) Who will be responsible for the initiation and control of training: HR specialists, line managers, employees themselves? What value is placed on the concept of 'self-development'?

(f) When, where and how will training activity take place? What mix of methods, formats and styles will be used?

(g) How much investment is the organisation prepared to put into training, development and organisational learning?

(h) How is training and development to be monitored and evaluated?

We will discuss various policy issues in detail in Chapter 2.

3.5 Learning, training and development

It may be worth distinguishing between these terms, although in practice they are often used interchangeably.

Definitions

> **Learning** is the process whereby people acquire knowledge, capabilities and skills
>
> **Training** is the use of planned, systematic instruction and other learning events and programmes to promote learning, with the particular aim of enhancing competence in a work role
>
> **Development** is the growth of people's knowledge and capabilities and the increasing fulfilment of their potential, through a range of learning experiences.

Development is often linked to systems whereby people gain experience within an organisation and are offered increasing opportunities and challenges through lateral or vertical movements in the organisation structure. 'Management development', for example, often implies not only management education and training, but mentorship and career planning, promotion planning and planned managerial succession.

3.6 Management development

Definition

> **Management development** is 'an attempt to improve managerial effectiveness through a planned and deliberate learning process'.
>
> (Mumford, 1994)

Much of our discussion of learning and training in Chapter 2 will apply as well to managerial as to non-managerial grades of staff. However, organisations have a significant investment in their managers – and in the quality of their leadership and decisions – and in order to secure and maximise the managerial resource, attention is typically given to:

(a) Some form of management education and training. This may range from short skill-based training courses (eg in leadership or interpersonal skills) to on-going learning activities directed towards demonstrating competencies (as defined by in-house or nationally-accredited competency frameworks) to sponsorship/leave for studies towards formal qualifications such as an MBA degree.

(b) Planned **career management**, to enable managers to gain experience of different functions, units or areas of the business, different national cultures (if the organisation is international or internationalising) and increasing levels of responsibility

(c) **Performance management** to develop and reinforce managerial competencies through on-going goal-setting and continuous improvement.

(d) **Self-managed and experiential learning**, encouraging managers to recognise and seek out opportunities to enhance their skills.

(e) **Guidance and mentoring** by effective motivators, success coaches and power sources in the organisation (usually more senior managers).

Activity 8 **(5 minutes)**

Suggest three reasons why an organisation should give attention to management training and development.

INTERNATIONAL COMPARISONS

- **European** approaches have traditionally been less concerned with management development as a discrete activity. In France, the making of a manager begins within the higher education institutions and forms part of the development of a historical social elite. In Germany, the approach is more functional: managers tend to stay in functional roles longer, and specialist expertise is pre-developed within the vocational education system. Where there is training, it tends to be highly structured and specified. Despite this 'relatively weak tradition in explicitly focused forms of management', there has been an upsurge of interest in management education since European Union: the emergence of business schools, MBA activity, and EU-led initiatives promoting the exchange of European business and management students between nations.

- The development of managers in **Japan** (based on a system of commitment and seniority), is long-term, slow-progression, carefully planned and generalist in its scope. 'Whereas Anglo-Saxon models stress individualism and development through short, intensive bursts of training to prepare managers for assignments characterised by challenge and risk, Japanese development programmes are longer and more culturally reflective in focusing on collectivism and group/team effort ... Unlike the US/UK where management development is in the hands of specialists, the Japanese view the relationship between the individual and the boss as a significant factor in developing the manager.'

(Beardwell & Holden, 1997)

So far, we have discussed learning theory mainly in terms of **individual** ***learning. We will now look briefly at*** **organisational** ***learning.***

4 THE LEARNING ORGANISATION

4.1 The learning organisation

Definition

> A **learning organisation** is one that facilitates the acquisition and sharing of knowledge, and the learning of all its members, in order continuously and strategically to transform itself in response to a rapidly changing and uncertain environment, and to develop and refine the capabilities required for future success.

A learning organisation values the process of learning – not just its specific outcomes. It learns how to learn: how to be open to new information; how to use feedback to adjust performance; how to view mistakes and failed experiments as opportunities for change; how to make decision-making flexible in order to accommodate learning.

Pedler *et al* (1991) define a learning organisation as one 'which facilitates the learning of all its members and continually transforms itself'.

This implies an underlying vision for organisational learning and flexibility, and the creation of a culture conducive to learning, via an integrated and mutually-reinforcing set of policies, processes and techniques.

An important aspect of the culture of the learning organisation is that learning is seen as a continuing process, both for the organisation and for the individual. This leads to organisational provision for **continuous learning and development**.

4.2 Learning culture

The cultural mechanisms and characteristics of a learning organisation are as follows (Senge, 1990; Garvin, 1993).

(a) Decision-making procedures are continuously modified in the light of experience, avoiding rigid plans and procedures.

(b) Problem-solving is systematic and based on scientific method rather than guesswork: insisting on data rather than assumptions, generating and testing hypotheses.

(c) Experimentation – the systematic search for and testing of new knowledge – is encouraged, in order to generate new insights. Continuous improvement programmes (based on the Japanese concept of 'kaizen') are a feature of learning organisation.

(d) Risk-taking, failures and mistakes are regarded as useful input to the learning process, to avoid problems in future. (This has been called the 'Santayana principle' after the philosopher who said: 'Those who cannot remember the past are condemned to repeat it'.) In any case, if something isn't working, it is better to experiment with something new than to stick with what you know for fear of failure.

(e) Information and feedback is encouraged from all possible sources (notably customers and competitors): opportunities to learn from others should be sought out. This includes the process of benchmarking: identifying best practice in other organisations and transferring appropriately adapted elements of their practice to one's own organisation. (Also known as 'SIS' – 'steal ideas shamelessly'!)

(f) Knowledge is disseminated throughout the organisation by formal communication and informal networking. Everyone operates with the knowledge of environmental changes and challenges and customer demands. Open-channel upward, downward and lateral communication is encouraged.

(g) Everything is open to challenge and questioning: no body of knowledge or procedure becomes 'enshrined' by habitual acceptance. Management actively supports questioning by subordinates.

(h) Selection, training and development, appraisal and reward are based not on existing goals and attainments but on flexibility, continuous improvement, initiative and ability to identify and exploit new areas of activity.

(i) Flexibility of decision-making is supported by self-managed team-working and the role of the manager/supervisor as coach/facilitator.

(j) Training focuses on 'learning how to learn': how to obtain, use and adapt to new information.

Activity 9 **(45 minutes)**

From what you know of how organisational culture is developed and reinforced, and building on the characteristics listed above, what would you expect to be the potential **barriers** to the creation of a successful learning culture?

4.3 The organisational learning cycle

According to the New Learning for New Work Consortium's report *Managing Learning for Added Value* the goal of the new learning paradigm is a workforce capable of taking responsibility for adding value. This amounts to a new learning cycle, which may be illustrated as follows (Figure 1.3)

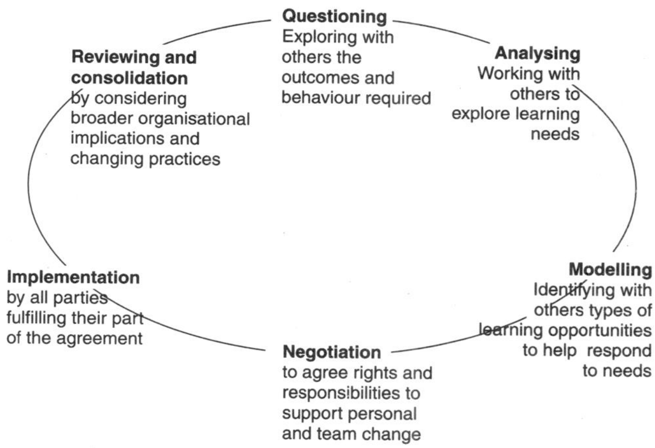

Figure 1.3: A new learning cycle – managing learning to add value

4.4 Individual ownership of organisational learning

Definition

> **Personal development plans** (PDPs) are action plans for individuals' skill and career development which put the onus on the individuals themselves to seek out and organise training and development opportunities.

Negotiated Personal Development Plans (PDPs) or **learning contracts** are often the basis of continuous development programmes. A PDP is usually prepared by the individual and his or her line manager (although they may ask a mentor or learning and development adviser for guidance); they retain responsibility for the plan and for the learner's progress.

Parsloe & Wray (2000) suggest that the role of the mentor or HR adviser will be to:

(a) **Confirm the PDP**: providing guidance in its preparation, checking that learning goals are realistic and effective, and helping to identify learning needs

(b) **Encourage the self-management of learning**: offering information about learning opportunities and encouraging learner in accessing them

(c) **Provide support during implementation**: providing guidance, feedback and resources as required

(d) **Assist in evaluation**: encouraging the learner to arrange formal evaluation with the line manager or qualification supervisor, and encouraging on-going development planning.

The most popular PDP schemes take account of people's wider needs and aspirations, rather than focusing on skills required for present job performance.

This trend is also reflected in **employee development programmes** which offer employees a wide range or 'menu' of development opportunities, not necessarily related to the job. The effect of such schemes is to develop a culture in which learning and adaptability is valued, as well as to attract, retain and motivate skilled employees.

EXAMPLE

A National Health Service development programme for unit general managers includes a budget for each individual to spend – as he or she wishes – on personal development. This can be spent on courses, seminars or books, or on 'buying in' a coach or instructor, or visiting other organisations to observe their methods – whatever. This approach empowers would-be learners, and encourages creative thinking about development needs and opportunities.

FOR DISCUSSION

Why might an organisation wish to give control of the development agenda to the individual employees? What might the drawbacks be? Who controls your learning objectives and opportunities?

Chapter roundup

- There are three basic theoretical approaches to learning: the behaviourist, cognitive and social learning approaches.
- Learning has been modelled as:
  - Four stages (unconscious incompetence, conscious incompetence, conscious competence, unconscious competence
  - A curve, showing the relationship between learning time and level of competence: training must take account of the steepness of the curve and the need for consolidating plateaux or steps.
  - A cycle, such as the experiential learning cycle of David Kolb (concrete experience, reflective observation, abstract conceptualisation, active experimentation): this can be used as an aid to self-managed learning.
- Transfer of work learning to the work context may be achieved in various ways, depending on the nature of the learning, the motivation and preferences of the learners and the support given by the worksite and work group.
- Honey and Mumford identified four learning styles: theorist, reflector, activist, pragmatist. Learning programmes should take into account the strengths and weaknesses of each style, as well as challenging learners to increase their learning repertoire and flexibility.
- Training may be directed at the acquisition of skill, knowledge, competence, attitudes/awareness or employability.
- The planning, design, implementation and evaluating of learning events and training programmes will have to take into account:
  - The organisation's philosophy and expectations of human resource development, as set out in the HRD policy.
  - The needs, requirements and preferences of various stakeholders in development.
  - The implications of learning theories and styles.
- The learning organisation is one that is skilled at creating, acquiring and transferring knowledge, and at modifying its behaviour to reflect new knowledge and insights.

Quick quiz

1 What is an 'empirical' epistemology and a 'rational' epistemology?

2 Define the four stages of learning.

3 What is a 'plateau' in a learning curve?

4 What are the two approaches to transfer of learning, and what other elements are needed to support transfer to the work context?

5 What are 'whole' and 'part' learning?

6 Which of Honey and Mumford's learning styles shows a preference for the 'generalising/abstracting' stage of the learning cycle?

A Pragmatist
B Activist
C Theorist
D Reflector

7 Distinguish between skill, 'know-that', 'know-how' and competence.

8 List the potential stakeholders in a training event.

9 Outline an approach to management development.

10 List five methods of creating a learning organisation/culture.

Answers to quick quiz

1 *'Empirical'*: a theory of how people know things based on the belief that the human mind operates purely on information gained from the senses by experience. *'Rational'*: a theory of how people know things based on the belief that the human mind imposes organisation and meaning on sensory raw material. (see paragraph 1.1)

2 See paragraph 1.2.

3 The point at which progress levels off, due to the trainee's need to consolidate, correct, regain motivation or establish unconscious competence before moving on further. (para 1.3)

4 Correspondence of elements between the learning situation and applied context *or* transfer by principle, which allows general learning to be transferred to specific contexts. Worksite systems, tools and resources and support from the manager and work group. (para 1.5)

5 Whole learning: tasks are taught or modelled in their entirety. Part learning: tasks are broken down and taught and practised stage by stage, building up to the whole task. (para 1.6)

6 C (paras 1.4, 2.1)

7 See paragraph 3.1 for a full account.

8 Owners/managers of the firm; line managers of trainees; training managers; instructors/coaches; external training providers; training community. (para 3.3)

9 See paragraph 3.6.

10 See paragraph 4.2 for a full account.

Answers to activities

1 A full account of the implications of learning theory for training design, is given in the text following the exercise.

2 We have used the example of assertiveness training: you may have come up with others.

Stage 1. You have not heard of assertiveness, so you are not aware that you relate to people in a way that is either aggressive or passive: you simply relate in the way that seems natural to you.

Stage 2. You read about assertiveness, or someone feeds back to you that your style of relating is unhelpfully unassertive, or you realise that you hardly ever get your needs met without damaging relationships: you realise that your behaviour is unassertive.

Stage 3. You research and think about the principles of assertiveness, and remind yourself of them by sticking positive affirmation messages around your home and office. You apply the techniques of assertion consciously, having to remind yourself of the principles, using scripted responses, monitoring their effectiveness.

Stage 4. You naturally react in an assertive manner, without having to remind yourself or plan to do so.

3 (a)

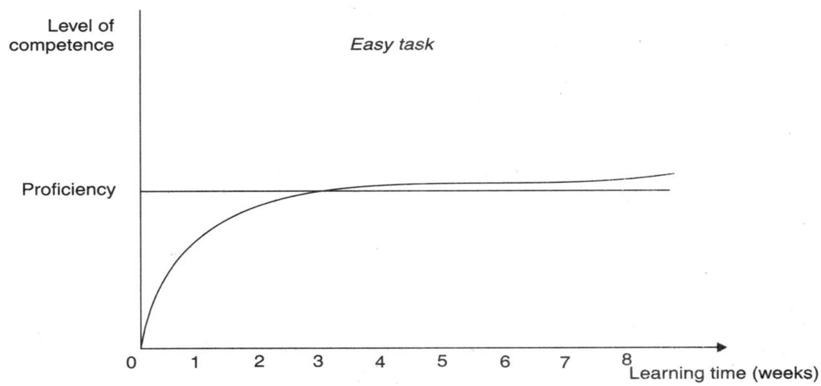

(b)

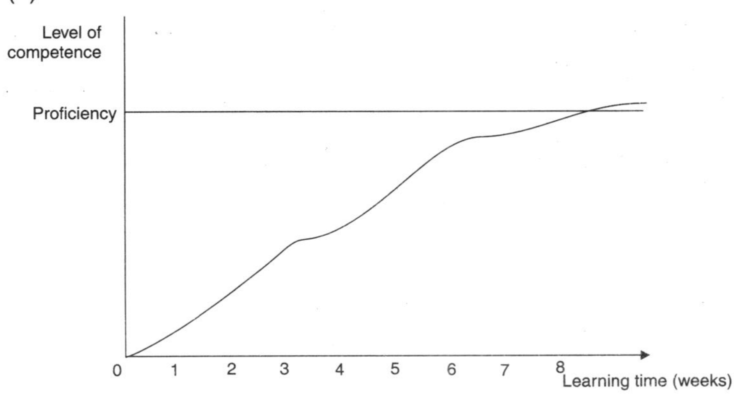

4 Some of the factors you may have identified include the following.

(a) Perceptual factors: unconscious incompetence, not seeing that there is a need; not receiving honest feedback from others

(b) Emotional factors: fear or insecurity about performance (not wanting to be a 'beginner' or 'learner'), fear of being judged, discomfort of conscious incompetence, frustration

(c) Motivational factors: lack of goals/incentives, unwillingness to take risks or make mistakes, no positive reinforcement for progress, previous bad experience with training

(d) Cultural factors: values about 'not getting above yourself', 'the way we do things here' frustrating application of learning; boss/colleagues/family unsupportive

(e) Physical factors: no suitable space or time to study, practise

(f) Situational factors: lack of training opportunities; poorly designed training courses (negative transfer, unsuited to learning styles of trainees)

(g) Skill factors: poor learning skills (never learned to learn), limited learning styles, poor communication skills

5 John is a pragmatist: Paula an activist: Ringo a reflector: Georgette a theorist. The course seems tailored to activists: reflectors would probably cope, but might not contribute enough to keep the classes going.

6 Assertiveness training is popularly seen as a prime means of remedying under-achievement in women, or of helping women to avoid exploitation at work. It is likely to be part of a 'Women Into Management' programme. The techniques and insights involved are likely to be of benefit to men as well, but it has been recognised that it is primarily women who are disadvantaged in western society by the failure to distinguish between assertion and aggression, submission and conflict-avoidance. Assertiveness training may help women to criticise, confront and direct male subordinates and colleagues non-aggressively. The failure of victims of sexual harassment to come forward may indicate another area in which assertiveness could be of value.

7 (a) It demonstrates that the individual is valued and believed to have potential.

(b) It gives the individual an enhanced sense of security (that he or she is and will be useful to the organisation).

(c) It can enhance a person's portfolio of skills, and hence a person's ability to take responsibility.

(d) It can motivate employees, because they see opportunities for advancement, or to make a difference to quality or innovation.

(e) Training and development sessions enable employees to mix with people from other business functions, and so develop networks and contacts.

(f) Training in areas such as assertiveness, communication or interpersonal skills can enhance personal effectiveness and self-esteem outside the work context.

8 (a) The prime objective of management development is improved performance capacity – both from the managers *and* from those they manage.

(b) Management development secures management succession: a pool of promotable individuals in the organisation.

(c) The organisation's showing an interest in the career development of staff may motivate them and encourage loyalty. (This will be especially important if the firm intends to rely on management succession to fill senior management positions.)

9 Some problems you may have identified include the following.

(a) Inadequate organisation mechanisms for multi-directional communication, training in learning, selection according to flexibility etc: these will have to be established, and old machinery (reporting channels, job descriptions etc) dismantled or adapted.

(b) Lack of commitment and example-setting by top management (essential to the development of culture).

(c) Poor communication and/or learning skills in some existing employees: they would need to be developed or the employees would need to be 'weeded out'. (This may happen through 'accelerated wastage', since the learning culture would be highly uncomfortable for them.)

(d) Organisational politics, discouraging the open sharing of information and acceptance of challenge.

(e) Fear/insecurity on the part of managers (required to open their decision-making to challenge) and all employees (fear of risk-taking, never secure in sense of competence under continuous improvement).

(f) Previous management style: punishing mistakes, avoiding risks etc.

(g) Lack of motivation to learn at all levels: inadequate perception of the need to be constantly learning, flexible – when it would be much easier to settle into established routines.

Chapter 2:
TRAINING AND DEVELOPMENT

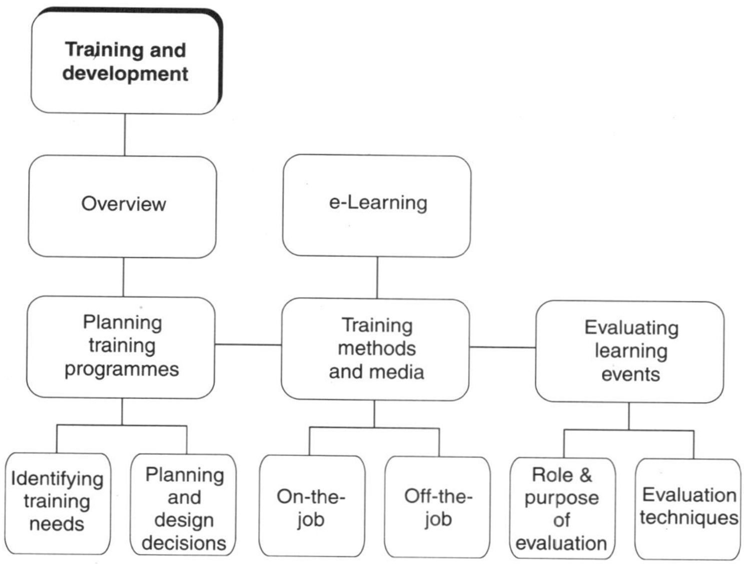

Introduction

In this chapter, we examine the practical application of the principles discussed in Chapter 1, starting with an overview of a systematic approach to training and development.

We discuss the key issues, resources and techniques of each stage of this approach, from the identification of training and development needs to the planning and design of learning events and programmes – and finally, the systematic evaluation of their success and contribution. This is a long chapter: take it at your own pace, and use the activities to consolidate your learning.

Your objectives

In this chapter you will learn about the following.

(a) The systematic approach to training

(b) The identification of training and development needs

(c) The setting of training objectives

(d) Planning issues in devising training programmes

(e) The advantages and disadvantages of on-the-job and off-the-job training and development methods

(f) The use of a variety of on-the-job and off-the-job methods

(g) The 'what, why, when and who' of evaluating learning events

(h) A range of models and techniques of evaluation

(i) How to investigate a vocational training scheme

(j) Implementation of (training) practice in the UK and one other country

1 OVERVIEW

If training is to make a impact on performance at an individual level, let alone at a strategic level, it must be carefully designed to suit the **need for training** and the **needs of the trainee.**

Definition

> According to the Department of Employment, **training** is 'the systematic development of the attitude/knowledge/skill/behaviour pattern required by an individual in order to perform adequately a given task or job.'

A systematic approach to training encompasses four basic stages.

Stage 1. Identify and define training needs

Stage 2. Design learning and development programmes which meet those needs, selecting relevant methods and media

Stage 3. Implement learning events and programmes

Stage 4. Systematically evaluate training (although this will not necessarily be a one-off, after-the-event exercise, as we will see in Section 4 of this chapter).

Training costs and the training budget

All instances and methods of training and development have costs associated with them and in any well-managed organisation, those costs will be subject to some form of budgetary control. Financial and other resources are likely to constrain what can be undertaken and must be considered in detail throughout the training management process.

(a) The budget may be set in advance and may limit the design and implementation of training.

(b) It may be possible to renegotiate the budget to reflect an urgent training need. Budget increases are most likely to be granted if the intended training outcome can be shown to be financially advantageous, so training managers will require an understanding of investment appraisal techniques.

(c) Training evaluation must include budgetary control elements. This may be confined to ensuring that costs have been in accordance with estimates, but, ideally, will demonstrate wider financial effectiveness (or its absence) in the form of a return on investment.

We will now look at each stage of the systematic approach in turn.

2 IDENTIFYING TRAINING NEEDS

2.1 Whose needs and objectives?

Training needs and outcomes should be evaluated in terms of their potential contribution to the key objectives of the organisation, which could include the following.

(a) Profitability; by increasing productivity/revenue or reducing costs

(b) The cost-effective provision of services, customer retention, ethical compliance, technical innovation, market standing and other measures of added value

(c) The survival or growth of the business, which may be based on profitability, return on investment for shareholders, retention of market share and so on

(d) Increased employee loyalty (with a knock-on effect in decreased labour turnover and smoother management succession)

(e) Enhanced corporate image (which may impact favourably on consumer attitudes and the ability to attract skilled labour)

(f) Enhanced potential for quality, innovation, flexibility in the face of change and acceptable risk-taking, through a culture of broad-based competence and support of learning.

There is no intrinsic incompatibility between a **business's** strategic goals for training, and the developmental aspirations of **individuals**. You will recognise from your studies in this area, the desire for learning, skill development and self-actualisation by the individual have long been recognised (Maslow, Herzberg) as incentives to motivated performance at work, as well as offering personal satisfaction.

Activity 1 **(20 minutes)**

When might fulfilling employee aspirations for training become incompatible with business objectives?

The training needs of individuals and groups vary enormously, according to the nature of the job and particular tasks, and the abilities and experience of the employees.

2.2 Training needs recognition

Some training requirements will be obvious and 'automatic'.

(a) If a piece of legislation is enacted which affects the organisation's operations, training in its provisions will automatically be indicated. Thus, for example, HR staff will need to be trained as and when various EU Directives are enacted in UK law.

(b) The introduction of new technology similarly implies a training need: for relevant employees to learn how to use it.

(c) An organisation seeking accreditation for its training scheme, or seeking a British Standard or International Standard (say, for quality systems, ISO 9000), will have certain training requirements imposed on it by the approving body.

Other training requirements may emerge in response to **critical incidents**: problems or events which affect a key area of the organisation's activity and effectiveness. A service organisation may, for example, receive bad press coverage because of a number of complaints about the rudeness of its customer service staff on the telephone. This might prompt an investigation which might in turn highlight the need for training in telephone skills, customer care, scheduling (for the team manager, if the rudeness was a result not of lack of skill but pressure of unmanageable workloads) and so on.

Some **qualitative indicators** might be taken as symptoms of a need for training: absenteeism, high labour turnover, grievance and disciplinary actions, crises, conflict, poor motivation and performance. Such factors will need to be investigated to see what the root causes are, and whether training will solve the problem.

Another alternative is **self-assessment** by the employee. This may be highly informal (a list of in-house or sponsored courses is posted on the notice board or intranet and interested employees are invited to apply) or more systematic (employees complete surveys on training needs). An example of a self-administered needs survey for managerial staff (suggested by Kramer *et al*, 1997) is as follows.

Self assessment of training needs

Please indicate in the blanks the extent to which you have a training need in each specific area. Use the following scale

Scale

1 __________ 2 __________ 3 __________ 4 __________ 5

(To no extent) (To a very large extent)

To what extent do you need training in the following areas?

Basic management skills (organising, planning, delegating, problem-solving)

A Setting goals and objectives
B Developing realistic time schedules to meet work requirements
C Identifying and weighing alternative solutions
D Organising work activities

Interpersonal skills

A Resolving interpersonal conflicts
B Creating a development plan for employees
C Identifying and understanding individual employee needs
D Conducting performance appraisal reviews
E Conducting a disciplinary interview

Administrative skills

- A Maintaining equipment, tools and safety controls
- B Understanding local agreements and shop rules
- C Preparing work flowcharts
- D Developing departmental budgets

Quality control

- A Analysing and interpreting statistical data
- B Constructing and analysing charts, tables and graphs
- C Using statistical software on the computer

The advantage of self-assessment, or self-nomination for training, is that it pre-supposes motivation on the part of the trainee and harnesses employees' knowledge of their own job requirements and skill weaknesses. The drawback, however, is that employees may be reluctant to admit to performance deficiencies.

A further alternative, therefore, is the use of **attitude surveys** and **360° feedback appraisal reports**, since the employee's superiors, subordinates, colleagues and customer contacts will be in a good position to identify performance deficiencies in areas that affect them: this will be particularly important in the case of customers.

Activity 2 **(15 minutes)**

Complete the above self-assessment for yourself. For any areas which are not applicable to your job, put NA (not applicable).

FOR DISCUSSION

Is a training course a 'perk' (or reward) – or a 'punishment' (or implied cirticism)?

Other training requirements may only emerge as a result of systematic learning gap (or training need) analysis.

2.3 Training needs analysis

Definition

Training needs may be defined as the gap between what people should be achieving and what they actually are achieving. In other words:

Required level of competence *minus* present level of competence = training need.

Training needs analysis may be carried out at the **corporate level** as part of the human resource planning process, through:

(a) Analysis of corporate objectives and business plans and their human resource requirements

(b) Analysis of existing human resource records and appraisals (training evaluations, performance management reports, surveys and so on)

(c) A human resources audit or skills audit, for a more comprehensive accounting of the current level of competence, skill, knowledge (and so on) in the workforce.

At **group/team and individual level**, a similar exercise will be carried out, to identify where the corporate needs can best be met.

The required level of competence for the job can be determined by:

(a) **Job analysis**, identifying the elements of the task in terms of key activities and outcomes

(b) **Skills analysis**, identifying the skill elements of the task, such as:

(i) What senses (vision, touch, hearing etc) are involved?
(ii) What left-hand/right-hand/foot operations are required?
(iii) What interactions with other operatives are required?

(c) **Role analysis,** for managerial and administrative jobs requiring a high degree of co-ordination and interaction with others

(d) **Existing records**, such as job specifications and descriptions, person specifications, the organisation chart (depicting roles and relationships) and so on

(e) **Competence analysis** or existing competence frameworks, such as NVQs relevant to the job, to define the skills, knowledge and competencies required to meet performance standards.

The present level of employees' competence (which includes not only skill and knowledge, but the employee's inclination or willingness to work competently as well) can be measured by an appropriate **pre-training test** of skills, knowledge, performance, attitude and so on. Performance appraisals and past training reports will furnish some of this information.

It should be noted that training needs analysis need not have a reactive or problem-solving focus, aimed solely at meeting shortfalls in competence in the current job. The **future development needs** of the organisation, team and individuals should also be taken into account, by considering employment, consumer and technological trends (such as the need to increase flexibility, improve e-commerce or customer service skills, or encourage innovation) and employees' potential for promotion, empowerment, multi-skilling and so on.

Training and development needs analysis should be part of the pro-active process of **performance management**, whereby managers and team leaders guide people in setting performance improvement and learning targets for the forthcoming planning period.

The training manager will have to investigate any gap between current and required performance/competence to see whether training might be the solution. (Remember, there are alternative solutions: machinery may need repairing or upgrading, poor motivation might need to be addressed through pay and incentives, and so on.)

If training is identified as the way to close the gap, a **learning or training specification** should be drawn up. This will include specific learning objectives, perhaps with action plans as to:

- Methods of learning that may be used
- Timescales within which learning should be undertaken and
- Methods by which achievement of the objectives will be monitored and measured.

2.4 Setting training objectives

Objectives should be clear, specific and related to observable, measurable targets. Ideally, there should be detailed definitions of:

(a) **Knowledge** – what the trainee should understand
(b) **Behaviour** – what the trainee should be able to do
(c) **Standard** – to what level of performance
(d) **Environment** – under what conditions.

The advantage of competence frameworks is that they typically define competent performance in exactly this specific and quantifiable way.

Objectives are the yardsticks that will allow the trainer (and trainees) to see clearly whether and how far training has been successful. They are usually best expressed in terms of active verbs: at the end of the course the trainee should be able to describe... , or identify... or distinguish X from Y... or calculate... or assemble... and so on.

It is insufficient to define the objectives of training as 'to give trainees a grounding in...' or 'to encourage trainees in a better appreciation of...': this offers no target achievement which can be objectively measured. Where possible, a **quantifiable** measure should be added: time taken to perform a task, percentage of questions answered correctly, percentage of errors acceptable, and so on.

Activity 3 **(30 minutes)**

Translate the following training needs into specific learning objectives. Begin each objective with the words: 'the employee will...'

Training need

(a) To know more about the Data Protection Act
(b) To establish a better rapport with customers
(c) To assemble clocks more quickly

Having defined what a training programme should be able to do, the training manager needs to evaluate different options for how training is to be delivered, and how the desired outcomes are to be achieved. We will outline some of the methods and media

available in Sections 4 and 5 below. Here, we will just highlight some of the decisions to be made.

3 PLANNING AND DESIGN DECISIONS

3.1 Training programmes and learning plans

Once organisational, job/role related and individual learning needs have been established, training managers must make plans as to the best route for implementation.

(a) **Training programmes** – a menu or 'core curriculum' of training initiatives which will be offered in the forthcoming planning period, which will be open to relevant categories of staff. Examples (Hargreaves and Jarvis, 2000) include:

- Finance training for project managers
- Management skills for all management staff
- Presentation and interpersonal skills for trainers, interviewers and customer service staff
- Teambuilding and teamworking for all departments
- Basic health and safety training for all staff
- Intra-departmental seminars and in-house discussion groups.

It may be necessary to design full-scale formal training programmes, if a suitably-tailored programme is not available 'off the shelf', or if large numbers of staff are regularly involved, making programmes more cost-effective.

Once these have been prioritised, they can be designed and timetabled.

(b) **Learning plans** – individual or team plans for accessing training courses/ resources and/or for taking advantage of learning opportunities at work. These may be more flexibly adapted to individual and team needs. Coaching, mentoring, reading and e-learning, for example, would not require formally designed programmes: learning targets, timescales and monitoring/ evaluation procedures would still need to be planned.

3.2 Type of learning

As we will see in Sections 4 and 5 below, learning experiences may be of different types, which will variously suit particular learning needs.

(a) **Formal and informal learning**

Formal learning often takes place away from the work setting, and involves techniques such as classroom teaching and instruction. It is driven by the teacher or trainer, often to a pre-set curriculum or agenda which may or may not be adapted to all members of the learning group. Transfer of learning may be difficult, although theorists may prefer this method.

Informal learning occurs in the workplace, in response to immediate, job-relevant needs. The learner essentially drives the process by asking questions and accessing opportunities for coaching, advice and instruction.

Since it is largely unplanned, it may not systematically meet training needs. However, some learners will find this method more relevant, more suited to their learning style and easier to apply in practice.

(b) **On-the-job and off-the-job learning**

On-the-job or workplace learning may use the workplace as a training environment (eg for briefings, demonstrations or site visits) or may use actual work processes and tasks as learning events. On-the-job training methods include: systematic job instruction; working with experienced colleagues or trainers; coaching or mentoring; and various guided challenges such as project or committee work.

Off-the-job training methods include: formal taught or self-administered courses (eg by computer-based training); outdoor training; research assignments and so on.

We discuss a range of these methods – and their advantages and disadvantages – in Sections 4 and 5 below.

(c) **Self-managed learning**

Individuals are encouraged to define their own learning objectives and create action plans (or Personal Development Plans) to meet them. Managers, mentors or trainers may jointly agree learning objectives, in the form of a **learning contract**. They may also guide the learner in accessing resources and learning opportunities, provide coaching, offer feedback as part of the evaluation process and so on.

(d) **Programmed learning**

The trainee works at his or her own pace through a carefully ordered sequence of learning modules and assessments. This is a feature of many distance learning and computer-based training programmes.

(e) **Blended learning**

Blended learning is a recognition that a mix of learning types, styles and technologies may be most effective in order to meet individual needs and learning preferences. This might be applied to a training course or programme: for example, using instruction on basic principles, group exercises for practice, e-learning for consolidation and coaching and mentoring for follow-up back in the workplace. Similarly, an individual's personal development plan might include a blend of reading, e-learning, experiential learning (using mentor feedback), coaching where required, and formal courses for certification.

Alan Mumford suggests that trainers should ask the following questions of any method proposed.

(a) What is the contribution of the method to the development of knowledge, skills and insight?

(b) What is the impact of individual learning-style preferences on the acceptability of the method?

(c) What are the particular features of this method that make it more appropriate than a method I have used previously?

(d) In what way is the method more appropriate than any other method for a particular need?

In addition, there is the need for cost-benefit analysis on any given method: are the outcomes to be gained worth the cost involved?

Activity 4 **(20 minutes)**

What methods of learning and training have you encountered in your job? What methods are you using now to study for your qualification? What do *you* think are the advantages and disadvantages of this 'blend' for you as a learner?

3.3 Timing and duration of training

If generic programmes, involving staff from different departments, are being planned, there are additional considerations for training managers.

(a) Negotiation with line managers as to the length of time staff can be available for training, when, and how the time could most conveniently be structured (day release, several-day blocks) to minimise the impact on the department.

(b) Consideration of the availability of training facilities and personnel (especially if external training partners are used): large-scale, specialist programmes may need to be booked up to a year in advance.

(c) Consideration of the learning curve and learning style preferences of trainees. Programme timetabling will have to take into account the need for icebreakers and participant teambuilding; refreshment and relaxation breaks; variations in 'pace' of learning activity to allow for consolidation, practice, reflection and so on.

There is a noticeable trend towards short-course or **'bite size' learning**, led by the Learning and Skills Council's (LSC) Bite Size campaign. Surveys suggest that training courses are increasingly modularised into 1-3 hour blocks – with two days considered a longer training course.

Key advantages of bite-sized learning are cost, time, the speed with which learning can be transferred to the job, and ease of learning. However, this is another area in which *blended* strategies may be required.

EXAMPLE

'There is widespread agreement that much of the demand for bite size is coming from employees. "Our courses are aimed at giving employees a few pragmatic techniques that they can use immediately. This was certainly an area where we found a demand and we knew that our employees were looking for more accessible learning," says [Louise Prashad, capability development manager at drinks company, Diageo].

'[The Diageo] training department has found that delivering shorter courses has enabled them to offer a wider range of topics. It has also eased some of the pressures on the training department. "Over 18 months ago we were struggling with the cost of three-day training courses, as well as trying to get people available for them." ...

'But the experience for the training department wishing to introduce modularisation can be challenging ...

' "One of the biggest challenges is getting the pitch right because of the short duration. There are restrictions on both the topic and the extent to which you can explore it in the short time allocated," [Prashad] told *PM*.

'In addition, it can sometimes be easier to get staff off-site for the whole day rather than an hour. "In some respects it is easier to arrange cover for one day than one hour. In a hospital, the loss of a person for an hour can be very evident in an emergency," says Simon Tisdale, head of training and development, Salford Royal Hospitals NHS Trust. ...'

(Roberts, 2003 (c))

3.4 Training providers

There is a wide range of options open to the HR or training department: see Figure 2.1.

	Advantages	**Disadvantages**	**Factors to be taken into account**
In-house options • 'On-the-job' vocational training (eg coaching) • In-house seminars, workshops, mentoring and job exchange for skill development • Participation in national initiatives, eg NVQs or Modern Apprenticeships • Call in a consultant to design and run specialist courses in-house	• May be cost-effective for large trainee numbers • Matching to specific organisational needs • Control over standards, accommodation etc • Ready transfer of learning to work context • Employer brand as corporate trainer	• Distractions from work task/context • Limited space, facilities, expertise? • Training department required to co-ordinate details (catering etc)	• Availability of suitably expert, trained instructors • Number of participants: cost of provision • Other alternatives • External advice and resources available
External options • Contract external training providers to run programmes externally	• Specialist facilities and expertise available • Less distraction from work tasks/ contexts • Greater freedom to raise work problems • Less demands on training department	• Expense • Planning/booking time required • May involve travel/ disruption for participants	• Cost – and resources available • Standard of training facilities • Qualifications, credibility and track record of trainers • Degree of specialism required • Location/travel/ access

	Advantages	Disadvantages	Factors to be taken into account
Distance-learning options • Published resources • CD-ROM/video resources • Software and web-based (e-learning) resources	• Learner-paced • Can be undertaken in own time/work or home • Cost advantages	• Lack of social interaction and support • Perception of 'own time' v 'work'	• Quality, interactivity and relevance of resources • Learning style preferences of trainees

Figure 2.1: Training and development options
Source: Hargreaves and Jarvis, 2000

3.5 Programme administration

A number of administrative matters will occupy the training department, including:

(a) Selecting participants for planned courses, according to preferences for schedule, content, learning style, location and training need priorities identified by line managers.

(b) Negotiating course content, time-tables and costs with external training providers.

(c) Booking external (and internal) training facilities and personnel.

(d) Sourcing relevant training materials and resources.

(e) Compiling calendars of training events, participant information briefings and other supporting materials.

(f) Marketing training programmes within the organisation.

FOR DISCUSSION

Beardwell and Holden (1997) quote the sad but familiar story of Del the Delegate, who returns from a course full of new ideas, anxious to implement them. He is confronted with scepticism and cynicism from both his bosses and fellow employees. 'The friction set up between Del and his company undermines his enthusiasm and exhausts all his energy. Del's behaviour reverts to what is (and always was) reinforced by the company.'

Is there an alternative ending to this tragic parable?

We will now go back and look at some of the available training methods and media in more detail. We will classify these under on-the-job training (Section 4) and off-the-job training (Section 5), but you should be aware that some methods may be used in either setting.

4 ON-THE-JOB TRAINING AND DEVELOPMENT

4.1 'Sitting with Nellie'

This is the traditional method of skill training. The trainee is placed beside an experienced worker (Nellie) and learns by observing her work and by imitating her operations and methods under close instruction and supervision, working with the actual materials and equipment that are involved in the job.

Advantages

- High transfer of learning (because learning is in context)
- Effective and economical (where the task is amenable to observation-imitation)
- Immediate feedback and adjustment
- Establishes working relationships as well as skills

Disadvantages

- Ineffective if 'Nellie' uses poor work technique, or the skill is not amenable to observation
- Ineffective if 'Nellie' lacks training/instruction skills and the job requires explanation
- Trainee is socialised into shop floor culture of work: not necessarily the methods or attitudes desired by management.

4.2 Job instruction training

This is a technique which can be added to the 'sitting with Nellie' approach to minimise the disadvantages cited above. It was developed as a guide to systematic on-the-job training, involving:

(a) Careful selection and preparation of trainer/'Nellie' and trainee: goals and objectives of learning outlined etc

(b) Full explanation and demonstration of skill/task by the trainer/'Nellie'

(c) Trial on-the-job practice/performance by the trainee

(d) Thorough feedback session between trainer/'Nellie' and trainee to appraise and adjust trainee's performance and set further improvement goals. (Repeat (b) – (d) as required.)

4.3 Coaching

Coaching is one element of the 'sitting with Nellie' approach, but may be used flexibly in a wide range of training situations, and at any time during performance on an on-going basis.

Coaching is on-the-job guidance, advice, correction and feedback-giving with a view to improving performance in specific skill areas. A coach should:

(a) Demonstrate how areas of a job are performed, and guide the trainee's own performance of the same tasks, by advice and correction

(b) Help the trainee to identify and resolve problems in his or her work

(c) Seek out or identify opportunities for the trainee to develop, through doing new things at work

(d) Give feedback on progress and results, to guide learning

(e) Encourage the trainee to assess his or her own progress and performance, and to formulate further plans for improvement in an ongoing cycle.

Essentially, coaching is a **collaboration** between the coach and the trainee, in which the coach's special role is encouragement and guidance as the trainee develops on the job.

Advantages

- Flexible and interactive: the pace and content of learning can be suited to trainee needs and trainer analysis
- Collaborative: involves trainee in problem-solving
- High transfer of learning (connected to live job performance)

Disadvantages

- Requires coaching skills
- Learning is limited to the abilities of the coach

4.4 Mentoring

Definition

> A **mentor** is a guide, ideally both more experienced and more powerful in the organisation, whose concern is the trainee's long-term personal development. The role is varied: counsellor, role model, champion/sponsor, spur to action or improvement, critical friend, encourager and so on.

While coaching is directed at short-term, skill-based development, mentoring is a longer-term relationship focused on broader career and personal development

A mentor should assist the 'mentoree' as follows.

(a) Help the trainee to greater self-awareness, by listening to, questioning and challenging his or her ideas, and feeding back on his or her behaviour

(b) Help the trainee to formulate and clarify his or her needs and ambitions in life, and to identify where events and opportunities at work fit into those plans

(c) Encourage the trainee to take responsibility for his or her development, while offering support – personally and within the organisation – if required

(d) Help the trainee to reconcile his or her non-work needs, interests and circumstances with the demands of work (or vice versa)

(e) Help the trainee to plan specific development and career paths or directions, offering opportunities where appropriate and possible

4.5 Action learning

Action learning is described (Pedler *et al,* 2003) as a method for individual and organisational development in which 'working in small groups, people tackle important organisational issues or problems and learn from their attempts to change things'.

The key elements of action learning programmes are as follows.

(a) A small group of four or five people (usually managers) meet together regularly, on a wholly voluntary basis, for the programme period (perhaps several months).

(b) Each participant brings a managerial or organisational problem they want to deal with.

(c) Group members support and learn from one another, acting as a mentoring, consulting and problem-solving network. (An external advisor may sit in and facilitate.)

(d) The group both generates and examines options in response to member issues/problems *and* learns about the interpersonal and managerial processes involved as they do so.

(e) Group members take action – and the group learns further from feedback on that action (in a learning cycle).

Pedlar *et al* note that many project teams, self-help groups, productivity improvement meetings and quality circles offer action learning processes.

So far we have looked at ways in which employees can acquire and improve skills in a particular job or task through guided imitation and practice. A slightly different approach is to give employees a 'taste' of different jobs and functions.

4.6 Training by switching or 'shadowing' roles

This may be accomplished by a number of methods.

(a) **Job rotation** or **'shadowing'**: the trainee is given several jobs in succession, to gain experience of a wide range of activities and departments. (Even experienced managers may rotate their jobs to gain wider experience; this method is commonly applied in the Civil Service.)

(b) **Temporary promotion:** an individual is promoted into a superior's position while the superior is absent. This gives the individual a chance to experience the demands of a more senior position.

(c) **'Assistant to' positions:** an individual with management potential may be appointed as assistant to a manager. In this way, the individual gains experience of management, without a risky level of responsibility.

(d) **Project or committee work:** trainees might be included in the membership of a project team or committee, to obtain an understanding of inter-departmental relationships, problem-solving and particular areas of the organisation's activity.

(e) **Assignments:** trainees may be delegated to a particular task or project by a superior.

Advantages

- Employees gain experience without risking immediate responsibility
- Task/role variety may increase job satisfaction and awareness of organisational processes
- Aids career/management/succession planning

Disadvantages

- May be perceived as perpetual traineeship: not real work
- May be perceived as a 'nuisance' in departments having to 'carry' trainees

4.7 Apprenticeship and traineeship training

Apprenticeships and traineeships involve a combination of on-the-job training (using any of the above methods) and off-the-job training (one or two days a week, or a number of weeks in the year, at a college or university). The trainees earn while they learn, but at a lesser rate than full-time employees of the organisation in which they are placed to gain their work experience.

4.8 Advantages and disadvantages of on-the-job training and development

On-the-job training is very common, especially when the work involved is not complex, but will only be successful under the following circumstances.

(a) **Assignments must have a specific purpose** from which the trainee can learn and gain experience; otherwise, it can be unfocused and overwhelming

(b) **It works best where the trainee is a practical type,** who prefers to learn by doing and can tolerate the process of trial and error. (Other people might need to get away from the pressures of the workplace to think through issues and understand the underlying principles before applying new techniques: remember Honey and Mumford's learning styles: how would they describe this type of learner?)

(c) **Trainers are themselves trained** in instruction and coaching techniques (as well as modelling efficient and effective work practices)

(d) **The organisation is tolerant of mistakes.** Mistakes are an inevitable part of on-the-job learning, and if they are punished or frowned on, the trainee will be reluctant to take further risks and will be de-motivated to learn.

There may be real risks involved in throwing people in at the deep-end: the cost of mistakes or inefficiencies may be high and the pressure on learners great. (Would you want medical procedures, or air traffic control procedures to be learned on-the-job?)

The key **advantage** of on-the-job training, however, is that it takes place in the environment of the job itself, and in the context of the work group in which the trainee will have to operate. The style of supervision, personal relations with colleagues, working conditions and pressures, the culture of the office/shop floor and so on will be absorbed as part of the training process.

Activity 5 **(20 minutes)**

If you have had work experience, list the advantages you experienced through on-the-job training. If you have not worked, think about this course and list the disadvantages of the different methods of study you are encouraged to undertake.

4.9 Self-development approaches

There are a number of techniques for informal, self-managed experiential learning at work.

- **Informal** – arising from the job and work context
- **Self-managed** – planned, implemented and evaluated primarily by the learner
- **Experiential** – using the learning cycle to turn any work event or action in to a learning opportunity.

There are various methods for self development.

(a) **Personal Development Plans** and **learning contracts** formulated with line managers or mentors: formal commitment to work towards specified learning goals, with action plans.

(b) **Personal Development Journals** or **learning logs**: a structured approach to the learning cycle. The learner selects a critical incident at work which illustrates a learning need: (s)he describes what happened, reflects on the event and its consequences, draws conclusions, and identifies future actions to reinforce successful behaviours and/or change unsuccessful behaviours.

(c) **Self-development groups**: groups which meet to discuss personal development and work issues, give each other feedback and information and so on – like a flexible action learning group.

Activity 6 **(no time limit)**

Keep a Personal Development Journal for a week.

(a) Select a particular skill area you want to develop: say, interviewing, presentation, assertiveness or team working.

(b) Each day, reflect on your day at work. What incidents demonstrate something to you about your competence (good or bad) in your chosen area?

(c) Describe the incident. What did you and others do or say? How did you feel?

(d) Reflect on the incident. What could you have done differently to get a better result? (Or what did you do *well*, to get a good result?)

(e) How can you put your insights into action? Plan to access whatever information, advice, feedback or help you need. (What will you need? Whom will you ask? When?) Plan a specific 'next time' to try your better solution.

***We will now look briefly at a particular kind of training programme, involving both off– and on-the-job elements:* induction.**

4.10 Induction training

From the first day in a job, a new recruit must be helped to find his or her bearings. There are limits to what any person can pick up in a short time, so the process of 'getting one's feet under the table' will be a gradual one. Induction is an ongoing process.

On the first day, a manager or HR officer should welcome new recruits. (S)he might discuss in broad terms the firm's rules and expectations, working conditions, pay and benefits, training opportunities and career opportunities.

The recruit's immediate supervisor should then take over the process of induction, which may cover areas such as following.

(a) Pinpoint the areas that the recruit will have to learn about in order to start work. Some things (such as detailed technical knowledge) may be identified as areas for later study or training, while others (say, some of the procedures and systems with which the recruit will have to deal) will have to be explained immediately. A list of learning priorities should be drawn up, so that the recruit, and the supervisor, are clear about the rate and direction of progress required.

(b) Explain the nature of the job, and the goals of each task, of the recruit's job and of the department as a whole. This will help the recruit to work to specific targets and to understand how each task relates to the overall objectives of the department – or even the organisation as a whole.

(c) Explain about hours of work and stress the importance of time-keeping. If flexitime is operated, explain how it works. Any other work practices, customs and rules should be explained clearly.

(d) Explain the structure of the department: to whom the recruit will report, to whom (s)he can go with complaints or queries and so on.

(e) Introduce the recruit to people in the workplace. (S)he should meet the departmental manager and all the members of the immediate work team (and perhaps be given the opportunity to get to know them informally). One particular colleague may be assigned to the recruit as a **mentor** for the first few days, to answer routine queries and 'show him (or her) the ropes'. The layout of the premises, procedures for lunch hours or holidays, rules about smoking or eating at work and so on will then be taught informally.

(f) Plan and implement an appropriate training programme for whatever technical or practical knowledge is required. Again, the programme should have a clear schedule and set of goals so that the recruit has a sense of purpose, and so that the programme can be efficiently organised to fit in with the activities of the department.

(g) Coach and/or train the recruit; check regularly on progress, as demonstrated by performance, reported by the mentor, and/or as perceived by the recruit. Feedback information will be essential to the learning process, correcting any faults at an early stage and building the confidence of the recruit.

(h) Integrate the recruit into the culture of the workplace. Much of this may be done informally: (s)he will pick up the prevailing norms of dress, degree of formality, attitude to customers etc. However, the supervisor should try to 'sell' the values and style of the organisation and should reinforce commitment to those values by rewarding evidence of loyalty, hard work and desired behaviour.

After three months, six months and/or one year the performance of a new recruit should be formally appraised and discussed. This should dovetail into a regular employee appraisal programme.

Activity 7 **(5 minutes)**

Did you have any form of induction into student life?

Compare your experience to the checklist given above. How effective did you feel your induction was? What difference did it make to your confidence in your studies?

We will now move on to off-the-job training.

5 OFF-THE-JOB TRAINING

5.1 Training providers

Off-the-job training providers include:

(a) Universities and colleges

(b) Private-sector colleges and training organisations, including assessment centres for group training exercises, and on-line or e-learning providers

(c) Training consultancies, which may help the organisation locate or develop courses to meet its needs

(d) Publishers of training materials (texts and workbooks, videos, computer-based training packages), or

(e) The in-house education and training department of the organisation itself (in large organisations).

Internal courses are sometimes run by the training departments of larger organisations. Skills may be taught at a technical level, related to the organisation's particular product and market, or to aspects such as marketing, teambuilding, interviewing or information technology management. Some organisations also encourage the wider development of staff by offering opportunities to learn languages or other skills.

One convenient and popular method of in-house education is **computer-based training** (CBT), **Interactive Video** (IV) or **e-learning** (Internet-based) using equipment in offices or even trainees' homes. Training programmes may be developed by the organisation or by outside consultants – or bought 'off the shelf': the software (or 'courseware') can then be distributed, so that large numbers of dispersed staff can learn about new products or procedures quickly and simultaneously.

EXAMPLE

'For years universities have been urged to become more businesslike. But the boot, it seems, is on the other foot as a growing number of employers attempt to emulate academia by setting up in-house "universities".

'Corporate universities take a variety of forms. While some are little more than revamped training departments, others represent ambitious attempts to co-ordinate learning and share knowledge across organisations. A few have even begun to imitate real universities to the extent of investing in academic research. But a common feature of many of these institutions is their use of academic terminology to describe, and raise the status of, corporate training and development activities.

'Although the University for Lloyds TSB was launched only last year, the corporate university concept is far from new. Pioneered in the US in the 1950s, it was not widely known in this country until the arrival of McDonald's Hamburger University.

'The fast-food giant has now quietly dropped this title in the UK and these days refers – more accurately – to its nationwide network of "training centres". But the Hamburger University is still going strong on the other side of the Atlantic, where corporate universities are set to outnumber traditional higher educational establishments by the year 2010, according to a report by the US Department of Labor.

'In the UK, the first homegrown corporate university was set up in 1993 by Unipart, followed two years later by Anglian Water's University of Water. But it is only in the past couple of years that the idea has really taken off. According to research by Ray Wild and Colin Carnall of Henley Management College, there are around 200 corporate universities in the UK, and this number is likely to increase over the next few years.'

Anat Arkin, *People Management* (12 October 2000)

5.2 Training methods

Some methods of off-the-job training include the following.

(a) **Training room instruction.** Similar to on-the-job job instruction training (see Paragraph 4.2 above), but in a dedicated training environment. Instruction is given using presentation techniques and/or a simulation of workplace equipment and methods.

(b) **Lectures** or **taught classes.** These are useful for knowledge or theory/principle-based learning. They may incorporate elements of instruction, case-study, role-play and other techniques to overcome the limitations of passive learning. They suit large numbers of trainees requiring the same basic body of knowledge. Drawbacks include their passivity and the difficulty of absorbing more than three or four key points per session, and their relative inflexibility to individual trainees' learning styles and needs.

(c) **Case study**. Using a description of a real-life scenario or example for analysis, providing insights and opportunities to exercise problem-solving skills, which can be transferred to the work context. Case-studies are a kind of on-paper simulation of work scenarios, allowing experimentation and exploration without risk. They are particularly useful for problem-solving and decision-making in a wide rage of specific contexts.

(d) **Role play.** The simulation of an interpersonal scenario, allowing trainees to experiment with learned behaviours and skills and to observe their effects in interpersonal encounters. This is particularly helpful in training for customer service, interviewing, conflict resolution and so on. It suits small groups, allowing for all-member participation.

(e) **Simulation.** In technical training, this may involve the mocking-up of equipment and environments so that trainees can experiment with technical skills and observe results in a safe, progressively-staged and controlled manner. (Flight simulators for pilots is one example.) In other forms of training, simulation may involve case studies, role plays, assignments of 'in-tray' exercises, which mock up typical tasks and scenarios to test trainees' organisational and problem-solving skills.

(f) **Open** or **distance learning.** Employees access technology-assisted instruction where and when it suits them, using training manuals, workbooks, video (and video conferencing for group sessions), tapes, computer-based packages and so on. Some face-to-face tuition may be used periodically to assess or reinforce learning, or to add more interactive and group work. This can be a highly economical method, especially where trainees are geographically dispersed.

(g) **Discovery learning.** A method by which trainees explore a task or concept for themselves, with relatively little initial instruction or demonstration. Trainees are thus encouraged to find out the key principles, constraints and methods of the task, and to ask the questions that are relevant to them. This is a highly trainee-centred technique which is tailored to the learning styles and needs of the trainees and fosters problem-solving and learning skills alongside specific technical competencies. It is, however, time-, labour– and cost-intensive.

(h) **Programmed learning.** A structure of learning by which a trainee, working at his or her own pace, works through a carefully ordered sequence of units or operations, each with objectives, instruction, testing and consolidation which allow the trainee to master one unit before progressing to the next. This is a feature of many distance learning and computer-based learning programmes.

(i) **Visits and tours**. Trainees are given opportunities to observe other sites, departments, operations and so on. This may be helpful in demonstrating:

how skills learned in the classroom are applied in practice; different types of machinery and work organisation; stages of operation before and after that in which the trainee will be involved; application of products/services by customers or end users; and so on.

(j) **Outdoor training**. Physical tasks and activities in challenging environments, designed to help trainees learn about themselves and their motivations, leadership skills, group dynamics and co-operation and so on. This is increasingly used in team-building and leadership training. Another growth area is corporate social responsibility (Allen, 2003), with teams being sent to renovate inner-city residential hostels and similar experiences, to encourage awareness of the wider community's needs. Learning takes place through the process of working out a group solution to a problem or challenge, with a facilitator aiding reflection and analysis afterwards. Outdoor training specialists are increasingly looking to target their offering more accurately, keeping courses short and making sure that they are useful (and clear) metaphors for the workplace.

(k) **Computer-based training.** Using computer software for instruction and assessment. (This will be discussed further below.)

(l) **E-learning**: learning or training delivered by electronic technology, particularly ICT developments such as the Internet and company intranets – in support of (rather than instead of) traditional training methods. This is a major development, and we will discuss it separately in Paragraph 5.4 below.

EXAMPLE

'Jaded employees? Perhaps its time to unleash the dogs of motivation. In fact, the Virgin Experience's "Thinking Like Canines" programme is not quite as barking as it sounds. Far from instilling dog-like obedience among staff, the basic aim is to strip bare the essentials of the workplace – that occupied by working border collies.

'Professional dog trainer Barbara Sykes, along with her team of canine consultants, takes participants through a variety of sheepdog trials – showing them their own communication foibles and how to get the best from individual team members. There is a strong focus on body language and presenting a clear message. "A dog will only respond to clearly defined body language, so each 'shepherd' learns to use their natural communication in different circumstances, with different recipients and under pressure," says Sykes.

'Within day-long programmes emphasising either leadership or teamwork, participants have to assess different dogs correctly and react to their personalities in order to realise each dog's full potential. Starting off in a training ring, they eventually graduate to the open field, where they are handed a variety of tasks with workplace parallels.

' "The dogs work together in harmony for the good of the pack," Sykes says. "They don't argue about their position and don't waste time scoring points off each other. They accept and respect leadership but use their initiative whenever the need arises." '

(Allen, 2003)

Activity 8 **(20 minutes)**

Suggest a suitable training method for each of the following situations.

(a) A worker is transferred onto a new machine and needs to learn its operation.

(b) An accounts clerk wishes to work towards becoming qualified with the relevant professional body.

(c) An organisation decides that its supervisors would benefit from 'picking up some ideas' on participative management and democratic leadership.

(d) A new member of staff is about to join the organisation.

(e) A supervisor allows himself to be intimidated by his work team and ends up carrying most of the workload himself. Occasionally, he tries to throw his weight around, but this never lasts.

5.3 Advantages and disadvantages of off-the-job training

Advantages	Disadvantages
• It allows exploration and experimentation by inexperienced employees without risking negative consequences for live performance	• If the subject matter of the training course is not felt to relate directly to the individual's job and organisation culture, the learning will not be applied afterwards, and will quickly be forgotten.
• It allows trainees to be away from the work environment where interruptions, distractions and performance pressure may interfere with learning.	• Individuals may feel that courses are, in general, a waste of time. They will not benefit from the training unless they are motivated to learn.
• It allows training to be standardised and distributed across a geographically dispersed workforce (eg via video, CBT or distance learning).	• Immediate and relevant feedback on performance and progress may not be available from the learning process, especially if knowledge is tested by unrealistic methods (such as exams) or at wide intervals. This will lower the learner's incentive and sense of direction.
• It allows for self-study at the trainee's own pace (eg via distance learning).	• It does not suit some people, who may not have much experience of (or taste for) classroom learning since school. Some people simply prefer a 'hands-on' type of learning: learning by doing.
• It may have organisational status as a reward or peak: being sent on a course is a sign of potential.	• Some organisational cultures encourage fear and insecurity around training courses, with the perception that a person sent on a course must be performing inadequately.

5.4 E-learning

Armstrong (2003) calls e-learning 'perhaps the most important recent development in approaches to the delivery and support of learning'. Surveys suggest that it is showing fast growth world-wide, with the UK becoming a major European market.

Definition

> **E-learning** is: 'Learning that is delivered, enabled or mediated by electronic technology for the explicit purposes of training in organisations. It does not include stand-alone technology-based training such as the use of CD-ROMs in isolation.' (CIPD)

This places e-learning firmly in the context of ICT networks, including:

(a) Networked computers forming a corporate intranet

(b) The Internet and World Wide Web.

E-learning systems typically include:

(a) **Software packages** – purchased 'off-the-shelf' from providers, or designed and developed in-house – which provide e-learning programmes and facilities: course content, navigation tools, interactive testing and feedback mechanisms and so on

(b) **Learning support** from online tutors and/or 'e-moderators', who track participation, co-ordinate information-sharing and interactions with other learners (discussion boards, chat sessions, student blogs, web seminars and so on) and provide guidance as appropriate.

In addition, **informal e-learning** may take place through everyday information-sharing and interaction over the Internet or intranet in the course of work.

Advantages and disadvantages of e-learning

Advantages cited for e-learning include:

- Learning at the learner's pace and convenience
- Flexible delivery, with access from home, work, libraries etc
- Reduction in delivery costs
- Potential for collaborative learning in 'virtual learning groups' for employees (and others) spread over wide geographical distances: chat, web conferencing and other technologies allow real time support and interaction
- High degree of interactivity, for immediate feedback (eg test scoring), question and answer and so on
- Potential for multi-media, high-interest presentation of learning material (not just 'e-reading') for enhanced learning motivation.

Disadvantages cited include:

- The need for Internet or network connection, which may not be available to all employees – and may be complex and expensive to set up

- The need for culture and attitude change to support e-learning, since it represents (for many people) a radically new way to work and learn
- The poor quality or relevance of some off-the-shelf e-learning programmes
- Limitations in the applications for which e-learning is suited, notably in the area of interpersonal skills. Over-reliance on e-learning alone has led to disappointed expectations.

Applications of e-learning

There are several areas in which e-learning might be particularly appropriate, because there are easily identifiable knowledge/learning needs which can be effectively met by electronic means.

(a) **Training in IT skills**. Learners can be led through relevant programmes, shown what to do, given opportunities to practise, tested and given competence feedback and records with little need for interpersonal or face-to-face support. Online support usually takes the form of e-mail contact and response.

(b) **Information/awareness-based learning**: induction briefings, health and safety awareness programmes, job-related information briefings/updates, new product/service information, company policy/rule changes and so on. E-learning does information transfer efficiently and with potential for greater creativity, interest and user-friendliness than oral briefings or printed manuals. Face-to-face methods might be used to follow-up or reinforce learning: emphasising the importance of compliance, say, or getting a team together to discuss the new product they've been informed about.

E-learning is not an optimal stand-alone solution for training needs such as 'soft' people management and interpersonal skills: negotiating, giving presentations, team-building, interviewing, leadership and so on. Instructor-led training, coaching, practice and feedback are required. E-learning may still be used to provide pre-course instruction and orientation, however, in order to reduce face-to-face time requirements. It may also be used where necessary to reach geographically dispersed learners: webcasts and video-conferencing can be used to stage virtual meetings and presentations, for example.

However, the limitations of e-learning in these areas have supported the use of blended learning: reinforcing e-learning with the right mix of face-to-face training methods (and *vice versa*).

EXAMPLE

'Over 2,500 **Royal & Sun Alliance** (R&SA) staff will undertake up to 35 hours of e-learning this year developing the IT and people skills that will support their customer facing role. As Katherine Plant, training manager at R&SA, explained: "In the past, with the numbers of people who need training, we would probably have implemented a classroom-based roll-out. My remit, however, has been to look at alternative methods of delivering this training and clearly *e-learning* is the best solution. We can ensure a consistent, high quality training message every time, wherever our people are located. It's also available to people when they need it and this latest learning technology shows them how much we are investing in their development; it sends the message that as a company we believe in both our people and our customers."

'The first of the three Customer Relationship Management (CRM) training programmes focuses on communication skills and includes the theory of how people communicate. It then looks at the practical skills required to put people at their ease such as how staff can match their pace and their language to that of customers.

'The second e-learning programme considers the rationale behind CRM at R&SA ... This programme recognises that the real experts in the business are its front-line staff and it encourages them to contribute their ideas and make the case for how these ideas could make a difference to their customers.

'The third e-learning programme will educate users on the new single view system which R&SA is implementing and which will underpin all customer contact. This is the system that maps and records all customer enquiries and interactions and ensures that all R&SA's staff have the latest customer details at their fingertips.

'Throughout the programmes R&SA is supporting its people with coaching and role-play exercises. This is the important "*blended solution*" aspect of the programme where staff can build their skills, get the objective feedback they need and learn from one another. With such people skills it is seldom a matter of right and wrong; people have their own ways of communicating and they need to develop their own style. The coaching input enables them to build awareness of what they currently do and develop the "best practice" skills and techniques that they have learned to ensure that their customers get a great service. This is what ongoing coaching and support is really about – helping people to develop their confidence and competence in their role.'

(Clague, 2004)

Activity 9 **(no time limit)**

Check out some e-learning related websites and browse through the links and resources.

- **www.e-learningcentre.co.uk**
- **www.e-learningnetwork.org**
- **www.smartforce.com**

How easy was this information to access and use? What does this say about e-learning?

We will now go on to the 'final' stage of systematic training: evaluation.

6 EVALUATING LEARNING EVENTS

6.1 Purposes of evaluation

Evaluation is the process whereby feedback is gathered on the progress and outcomes of training events or programmes, in order to support further planning and decision-making. It may fulfil a number of purposes.

(a) To **determine the effectiveness of training**: measuring whether each training programme is meeting its intended objectives (in terms of learning outcomes, stakeholder satisfaction, impact on performance and a range of other criteria). Effective evaluation is important to validate training as a business tool for improving organisational performance and profitability.

(b) To **help improve the design of training**: asking 'Are we training the right people in the right things, in the right way, with the right materials, at the right time?'

(i) Identifying the strengths and weaknesses of specific training approaches, activities, materials and providers, so that programmes can be revised or modified for improved value and benefits.

(ii) Identifying what types of staff benefit the most or the least from a given training approach, in order to adjust and develop future programmes and select appropriate participants

Effective evaluation enables training designers and providers to make objective comparisons and decisions.

(c) To **support accountability:** determining the cost-benefit ratio or return on investment of each training event (and of training activity as a whole), in order to justify expenditure – and gain the support of management and other training sponsors, in the face of competition for scarce resources.

(d) To gather information on the nature, experience and outcomes of training programmes so that they can be effectively **marketed within the organisation**

(e) To allow **stakeholders** in the training process to express their needs and preferences and to have their feedback heard, in order to improve the relevance and acceptability of training

(f) To provide **management information**: on skills and competences (for HR planning), training costs, benefits and resources (for HRD planning) and so on.

6.2 What should be evaluated?

In one sense, the 'what' of evaluation refers to the **criteria** for measuring training success: what are evaluators looking *for*? There are various models suggesting specific sets of criteria, which we will discuss in Paragraph 6.6. However, the full range of criteria selected for evaluation might include the following.

(a) **Participant reactions**: trainees' satisfaction with the course or activity, its relevance to their work and so on. This can be measured using feedback forms, attitude surveys or 'happy sheets' (and also, as a rough guide, numbers of trainees applying for and attending training events). It is important, because a negative experience may inhibit transfer of learning, cause negative word-of-mouth and impact on future take-up of training opportunities.

(b) **Learning outcomes**: new or enhanced knowledge, skills and attitudes. This can be measured using post-training tests or assessments (and follow-up tests to see how much has been retained after the training is over). The effectiveness of a training event may be measured by the number of participants achieving learning objectives.

(c) **Behaviour change**: new work behaviours which reflect learning outcomes, by applying new skills or awareness on the job. This can be measured using observation and performance monitoring, both before and after training (for comparison). It is important in order to evaluate transfer of learning.

(d) **Performance change**: the outflow of behaviour change into impact on individual, unit and organisational performance. This can be measured using feedback from the performance management system (on key performance indicators), and comparing groups who have and have not been through the training. (Otherwise, it is hard to verify that training has made the difference, rather than a number of other variables.) This is important to make a business case for training.

(e) **Other desired outcomes**: for example, whether training has been effective in encouraging networking and co-operation between participants (particularly if they have been brought together from different units or dispersed teams); or whether training is perceived as a valued benefit or reward (if this is part of the organisation's reward management plans).

(f) **Costs of training**: in order to compare the cost-effectiveness of different approaches and providers, and to provide data for cost-benefit (or return on investment) analysis. The organisation should measure both:

- **Direct** costs, which would not be incurred if the particular training did not take place: the cost of learning resources and materials; external training facilities and trainer/consultant fees; travel expenses and so on *and*
- **Indirect** costs, which would be incurred whether or not the particular programme was held: training department salaries and costs, participant salaries for the duration of the training, in-house training facilities and equipment.

(g) **Efficiency**: the amount of learning achieved relative to the amount of time and effort expended. This is an important element in cost-effectiveness.

(h) **Performance to schedule and specification**: the performance of the training provider in relation to agreed criteria for training completion dates, support services, quality of materials and facilities and so on.

In another sense, the 'what' of evaluation refers to the activities and attributes to be assessed: what are evaluators looking *at*?

Activity 10 **(5 minutes)**

What areas would you look at in order to evaluate the quality and suitability of a training course – both as a learner and as training manager?

6.3 When should evaluation take place?

Evaluation is a decision-making tool. It should lead to decisions about which programmes will be continued or discontinued; which learning methods and activities will be incorporated; which materials and technologies will be used; which course providers and learning facilitators will be used; who should be encouraged to participate and so on. In a sense, therefore, the four 'stages' of systematic training should really be seen as a **cycle** (Bramley, 1986), whereby information from the evaluation stage is fed back into further analysis of training needs, design decisions and programme plans: Figure 2.2.

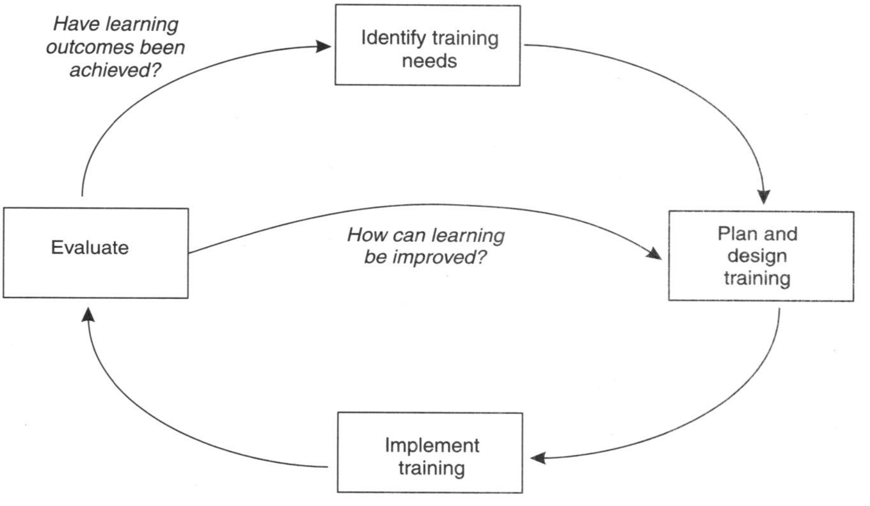

Figure 2.2: Systematic training cycle

There are two basic types of evaluation.

(a) **Formative** (or process) evaluation focuses on appraisal as a source of data which will be fed back into the planning process, in order to refine or improve training. It may be carried out:

- At the development stage, in order to check that the planned approach, activities, content and materials are likely to achieve the desired training outcomes and justify their anticipated costs.
- On an on-going or periodical basis throughout the training programme, in order to highlight any problems or shortcomings which need adjustment.

(b) **Summative** (or product) evaluation focuses on appraisal of the effectiveness of the completed event or programme, at its conclusion. The 'product' or results of the programme are analysed and recommendations made as to whether the programme should be continued and/or modified in future.

Both types of evaluation are necessary. Formative feedback is particularly beneficial because it helps training providers to get things right *this* time – not just next time! This in turn helps to ensure the least possible waste of time and resources.

6.4 Who should evaluate training?

We noted in Chapter 1 that there are a number of stakeholders in training. All of them will want to carry out some level of evaluation in order to justify their particular 'investment' in the training. The roles of key stakeholders in the evaluation process may be summarised as follows.

(a) **Senior management** will undertake a strategic-level evaluation of training as a whole, both formative (in order to approve the human resource development plan and resources) and summative (in order consider the business case for further or adjusted plans). Information about the impact of training on overall organisational performance and culture may only be available at this level.

(b) **Training/development specialists** will have the primary responsibility for evaluating particular training programmes and events, in order to design and manage programmes effectively, justify past and future expenditure, and supply management information for the higher level. Evaluation criteria, methods and schedules should be built into all training plans. Those who deliver formal training will have an interest in feedback on their performance.

(c) **Trainees** have an important role in evaluating training events in which they have participated: trainee satisfaction is a key criterion, because it supports effective learning and transfer of learning. Trainee feedback *during* training is particularly valuable, as it helps trainers to adapt activities as far as possible to the needs and preferences of the current participants: trainees should be encouraged to co-operate with trainers in improving their experience and outcomes – rather than complaining at the end. In addition, feedback may be sought on the wider perception of training by employees, which will influence its take-up (where voluntary), effectiveness (which depends on learner motivation) and usefulness as part of the total reward package.

(d) **Trainees' line managers** have a strong interest in the transfer of learning to the workplace. Their main role in evaluation will be to assess the impact of training on work behaviour and individual/group performance, as a key criterion of training effectiveness.

(e) **External training providers** will need to evaluate their own performance in relation to desired outcomes: number of courses run, number of students, income, profitability, reputation, client/trainee satisfaction and so on. They should make use of feedback from their customers (both training managers and trainees) and should provide feedback to them (eg trainee test and assessment results, and perhaps also a report on the conduct or motivation of trainees).

6.5 How is evaluation data gathered?

A number of formal and informal evaluation techniques may be used, as shown on the next page.

FOR DISCUSSION

Have you ever been asked to fill in a feedback or review sheet for a training event or materials? How seriously did you take this exercise? What might prevent students or trainees from taking the feedback process seriously (or engaging in it at all)? What kinds of questions could be asked to give planners and providers *meaningful* feedback to help them improve training?

Method	Advantages	Limitations
Interviews		
• With participants, line managers, team members, trainers • To assess satisfaction, learning, impact on work performance	Flexible focus and style Opportunity for clarification, probing Face-to-face: may encourage personal feedback (eg on aspirations, problems)	Time/labour-intensive Costly May be unstructured Face-to-face: may inhibit honest feedback May 'lead'/influence responses
Questionnaires		
• 'Happy Sheets' (reaction or satisfaction focused) • Systematic evaluation instruments (reaction, outcome and improvement focused)	Low cost to administer May be tailored to specific events May allow anonymity, more honest responses Respondents control pace and depth of feedback	If badly designed or managed: poor data quality and return rate Data may be too general Questions may focus on 'likes/dislikes' rather than learning achieved, content relevance and how trainers/materials/facilities supported learning (or not)
Direct observation		
• Of training (eg by assessors 'sitting in') • Of post-training behaviour	Good way to measure behavioural change Non-intrusive on personal responses	May be disruptive May be subjective: requires trained observers May influence behaviour
Written tests		
• Knowledge test (eg by multiple choice) • Case study analysis	Low-cost development Ease of administration Ease of processing/scoring (objective testing) Allows wide sampling	May not relate to directly to work: only measures cognitive learning May not reflect learning (eg due to test stress or literacy/language problems)
Performance tests		
• Competence assessment and certification • Simulation/in-tray exercises/role plays	Relevance to work and performance Includes cognitive and skill-based learning Allows evaluation of 'soft' (interpersonal) skills	Time consuming to create, administer and score May require external development/assessment High cost

Method	Advantages	Limitations
Performance data		
• Individual performance records • Organisation and unit results such as sales, productivity, labour turnover, quality standards • External input, such as customer comments	Job-based therefore directly relevant Easy to review Historical: not influenced by evaluation process	Relevant records may not be available Records prepared for other purposes may not contain usable data
Training audit • Part of some schemes of organisational development or quality management	May provide both training needs assessment and training evaluation as part of audit process	Principally concerned with the existence and adequacy of systems and records such as skill requirements and certification

6.6 Evaluation models

There are a number of models of evaluation. The most influential is the Kirkpatrick Model, originally devised in 1959.

The Kirkpatrick Model

Kirkpatrick sets out four levels of evaluation.

Level	Evaluation of	Measure	Methodology
1	**Reaction**	Trainee satisfaction: 'Were participants pleased with the programme?'	Post-training forms, quantifying reactions as far as possible, and encouraging written comments and suggestions
2	**Learning**	The extent to which learning objectives were met: 'What did participants learn in the programme?'	Pre– and post-training written or performance-based tests of the materials covered in the training
3	**Behaviour**	Transfer of learning to the workplace: 'Did the participants change their behaviour based on what was learned'?	Various: eg observation, work/output sampling, follow-up training audit, competence assessment
4	**Results**	Impact on the organisation: 'Did the change in behaviour positively affect the organisation?'	Monitoring comparable pre– and post-training data: sales or productivity, accidents, customer satisfaction

The Kirkpatrick model is widely known and accepted. It usefully highlights key outcomes of training, the link between them and the need to evaluate all four of them. As Armstrong (2009) notes: 'Training produces reactions, which lead to learning, which leads to changes in job behaviour, which lead to results at unit and organisational level. Trainees can react favourably to a course... but learn little or nothing. They might learn something, but be unable or unwilling to apply it. They might apply it but it does no good within their own areas, or it does some good in their function, but does not improve organisational effectiveness.'

However, there are some well-recognised issues in applying this model.

(a) It can be interpreted as focusing on post-training or summative evaluation, rather than formative evaluation, for the purposes of programme design and inter-stage adjustments and improvements. Kaufman (1994), for example, separates Level 1 into 'enabling' (the availability of inputs for the training programme) and 'reaction' (participants' satisfaction).

(b) Many organisations evaluate only at the easiest and least costly Level 1: using 'smiles tests' which are meaningless in terms of justifying training's contribution (Level 4). Nor does enjoyment imply that trainees will apply what they have learned to their jobs: it may be seen as irrelevant, or may not be backed by managerial or resource support. Phillips (1997) adds a useful strand at Level 1 called 'intent to apply'.

(c) Level 4 is particularly difficult to evaluate in practice: it is not always easy to prove that improved results are attributable to training, let alone to quantify its contribution.

(d) Evaluation at all levels for all programmes may not be necessary or cost-effective. Training planners may find information from Level 1-2 feedback most useful in designing training events: obtaining information at higher levels of evaluation may appear both more costly and less valuable.

(e) Despite the widespread neglect of Level 4, the model in some respects falls short. Kaufman (1994) adds a Level 5 which addresses the broader societal outcomes of training (adding the wider community to the list of stakeholders). Phillips (1997) adds a Level 5 for Return on Investment (ROI) assessment, calculating a monetary value for the impact of the instructional programme.

FOR DISCUSSION

'The evaluation of training, like motherhood and apple pie, is inherently a good thing. but, because short-term priorities always crowd out their longer-term competitors, it's typically something we plan to do better next year – after all, we've got away with it so far, so another year won't hurt!' (Shepherd, 2004)

Why does a firm really *need* to evaluate its training programmes?

The CIRO model

The CIRO model (Warr, Bird and Rackham) sets out four evaluation categories.

Context Identify:

- The performance need/deficiency or desired outcome at which the instructional programme is aimed

- The specific changes in work behaviour that will overcome the deficiency
- The knowledge, skill or attitudes needed to change behaviour

Input Identify the resources to be used in conducting the programme

Reaction Measure the participants' satisfaction with the programme

Outcome Measure the results of the programme in terms of context requirements.

This more formative model uses similar *outcome* measures to the Kirkpatrick model, but broadens the scope of evaluation to include planning *inputs* including need analysis and resourcing. It does not offer an extensive framework for assessment (like the Kirkpatrick model or ROI) but it provides a strong linkage between the objectives of the training programme and its eventual outcomes, creating an objective basis for validation of the programme: did it achieve what it was intended to achieve?

Return on Investment (ROI) model

Definition

> '**Return on investment** (ROI) is a measure of the monetary benefits obtained by an organisation over a specified time period in return for a given investment in a training programme. Looking at it another way, ROI is the extent to which the benefits (outputs) of training exceed the costs (inputs).' (Shepherd, 2004)

Phillips (1997) put forward ROI as a quantitative measurement of training impact, stressing its use in justifying expenditure on a planned training programme (or training activity as a whole) and evaluating the extent to which the planned/desired return was achieved. It is seen as a 'Level 5' evaluation, not a substitute for measuring learner satisfaction, learning outcomes or learning transfer.

ROI is a complex process of data gathering and analysis. Phillips suggested that programmes suitable for ROI evaluation are those which:

(a) Involve large target audiences
(b) Are expected to have a long life cycle
(c) Are important to the strategic objectives of the business
(d) Require significant investment
(e) Have high visibility
(f) Are developed through systematic and comprehensive needs assessment.

A (deceptively simple) approach to calculating ROI (Shepherd, 2004) involves:

(a) Forecasting and/or measuring the **total costs** associated with a training programme (including evaluation costs).

(b) Forecasting and/or measuring the **total financial benefits** of the training programme. This is not easy, as many of the benefits of training are non-quantifiable and difficult to measure, and some may take time to emerge to the point where they offer a measurable return on investment: paradigm shifts and cultural changes, employee satisfaction and commitment, increased flexibility and ideas generation and so on. However, quantifiable categories include:

(i) Labour savings

(ii) Productivity increases

(iii) Other cost savings (eg fewer machine breakdowns and accidents, lower staff turnover)

(iv) Other income generation (eg higher sales success rates, new product ideas)

(c) **Calculating return on investment**:

$$\%\ ROI\ (over\ a\ specified\ period) = \frac{benefits}{costs} \times 100$$

(d) **Calculating the 'packback' period**: how long it will take before the benefits of the training match the costs and the training pays for itself. This is a powerful tool in marketing a training proposal to senior management – as long as the figure is relatively low!

$$Payback\ period = \frac{costs}{monthly\ benefits}$$

Activity 11 **(no time limit)**

Find out how training is evaluated in your own work organisation, or another organisation of your choice. (You may use published sources or personal contacts to obtain this information.) What model of evaluation is used (if any)? How effective is the method perceived to be? What limitations or difficulties are experienced in practice?

Chapter roundup

A systematic approach to training can be illustrated as follows.

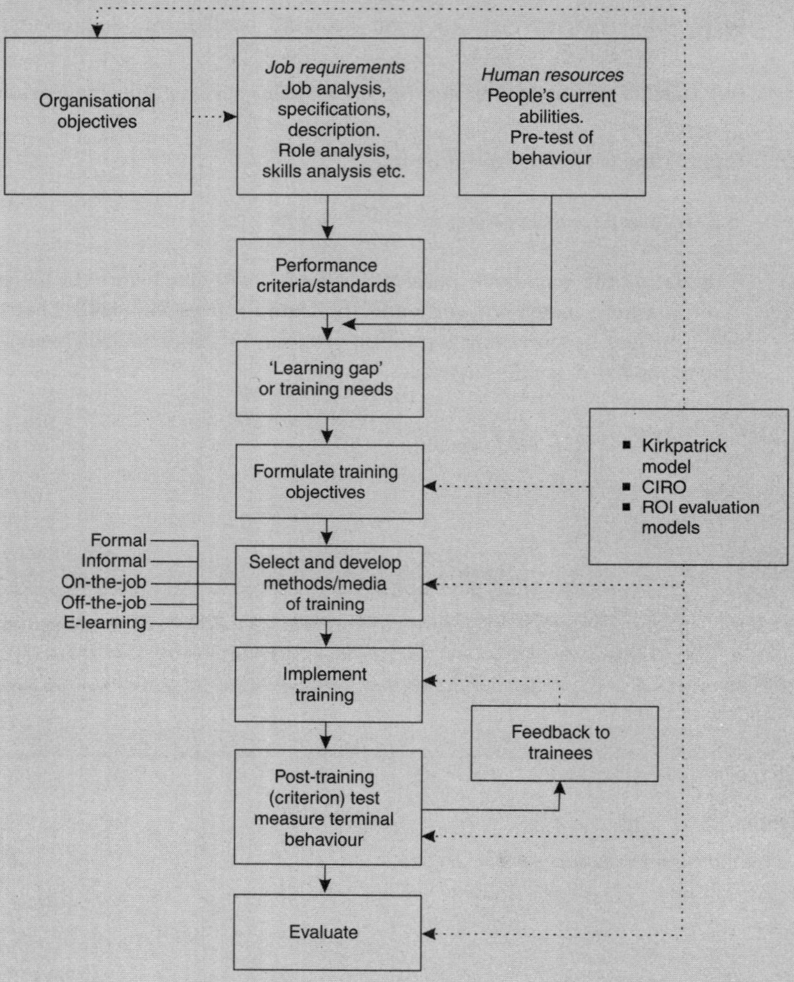

Quick quiz

1. How do 'training needs' arise in an organisation and how would you carry out a 'training needs analysis' if required to do so?
2. What is 'blended learning'?
3. List three methods of 'on-the-job' training.
4. What are the advantages and disadvantages of 'on-the job' training methods?
5. What is induction?
6. Training using physical challenges in unfamiliar environments is called 'Action Learning'. True or false?
7. Outline the advantages and disadvantages of e-learning.
8. Suggest three key reasons for evaluating training.
9. What criteria should be evaluated?
10. What do TKM, CIRO and ROI stand for?

Answers to quick quiz

1. The answer depends on the job or tasks and the abilities and experience of individuals or groups. Training needs analysis entails finding the difference between the required level of competence and the present level. (see paragraphs 2.2-2.3)
2. Using a mix of learning types, styles and technologies in order to meet needs and preferences of trainees. (para 3.2)
3. Coaching, job rotation, 'assistant to' positions. (paras 4.1-4.7)
4. The main advantage is that it is relevant to the job. It takes place within the job environment, so that the style of supervision, personal relations and working conditions are absorbed. The main disadvantages are pressure and the cost of mistakes. (para 4.8)
5. Introducing new recruits to the job and environment. (para 4.10)
6. False. (paras 4.5, 5.2)
7. See paragraph 5.4 for a full answer.
8. Determining effectiveness, improving design, supporting accountability. (para 6.1)
9. See paragraph 6.2 for a full answer.
10. The Kirkpatrick Model; Context, Input, Reaction, Outcome; Return on Investment. (para 6.6)

Answers to activities

1 Fulfilling such aspirations may become incompatible with business objectives if:

(a) Specific training outcomes become divorced from the strategic aims of the business, and become focused on purely personal development for its own sake

(b) Training outcomes serve to increase employee mobility, by giving them transferable skills and self-confidence

(c) Training outcomes encourage the employee to 'outgrow' the organisation's culture and leadership style, creating expectations and capabilities that the organisation may not (yet) be in a position to utilise or even tolerate

2 Your own needs assessment: you might make this the basis for Activity 11, later.

3 The answer offered by Torrington and Hall (1991) is as follows.

Training needs	**Learning objectives**
(a) To know more about the Data Protection Act	The employee will be able to answer four out of every five queries about the Data Protection Act without having to search for details.
(b) To establish a better rapport with customers	The employee will immediately attend to a customer unless already engaged with another customer.
	The employee will greet each customer using the customer's name where known.
	The employee will apologise to every customer who has had to wait to be attended to.
(c) To assemble clocks more quickly	The employee will be able to assemble each clock correctly within thirty minutes.

4 Your own experience. Note particularly how the *blend* of approaches gives you variety, suits your learning style and so on. Disadvantages may include inconsistent messages, extra time/cost and so on.

5 You have probably covered most of the following points.

Advantages include working for a specific purpose, carrying out practical work, the feeling of achievement when a task is completed successfully, knowing you have made a contribution to the organisation's objectives, learning to work with others. If mistakes are made they are rectified and do not affect your overall performance (unless you make too many or keep making the same mistakes).

Disadvantages could include the difficulty of relating exercises or assignments to the 'real work' situation, working mainly on your own and the few practical applications for your studies. Unlike work, you only have one chance to get things right: the marking system means that if you make a mistake there is little you can do once the work is handed in and marked.

6 We highly recommend this exercise: it may become a (very useful) habit!

7 Your own experience (NB: important source of learning!)

8 Training methods for the various workers indicated are as follows.

(a) Worker on a new machine: on-the-job training, coaching.

(b) Accounts clerk working for professional qualification: external course – evening class or day-release.

(c) Supervisors wishing to benefit from participative management and democratic leadership: internal or external seminar, or group training exercise. Careful attention will need to be given to how these 'ideas' will be integrated into practice on the job.

(d) New staff: induction training.

(e) Intimidated supervisor: assertiveness training.

9 Note that this activity was in itself an exercise in e-learning!

10 Evaluation would typically cover areas such as: the learning and teaching processes used; course content; materials and teacher aids; credibility and competence of trainers/facilitators; training premises and amenities; flexibility and quality of service; costs; and outcomes of training (according to the criteria discussed earlier).

11 Your research: good evidence of competence in this area!

Chapter 3:
LEARNING AND SKILLING INITIATIVES

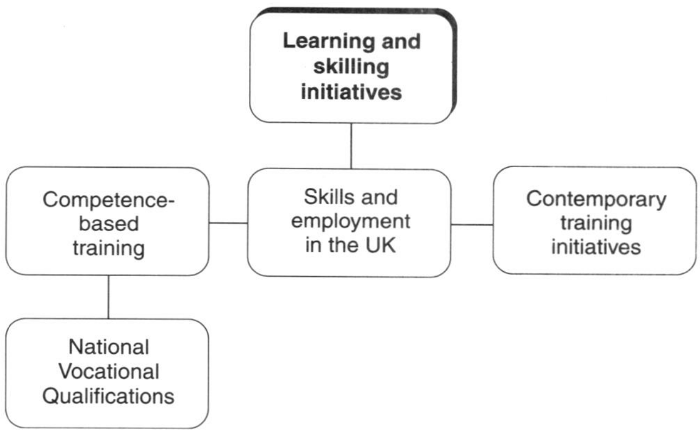

Introduction

One of the key resources of HR planners and developers will be contacts with other organisations dedicated to assessing, developing and mobilising employable skills. A wide range of schemes is sponsored in the UK by the Department for Children, Schools and Families, the Department for Business, Innovation and Skills and the Qualification and Curriculum Development Agency (QCDA) to support vocational education and training both in and out of the workplace, aimed primarily at:

- Helping redundant and other unemployed individuals to develop (or re-develop) vocational skills in order to find work; and
- Increasing the knowledge and skill base of the UK labour pool to support economic growth.

All these schemes will be relevant to HR practitioners looking to forecast skill supply in the local labour market; recruit suitably skilled individuals; demonstrate corporate social responsibility by creating employment and development opportunities; support the development and employability of existing employees; and/or ease the impact of redundancy on staff, where required.

In this chapter, we will look briefly at a range of UK training initiatives and their sponsors. Many initiatives and structures are still under development or being reviewed. Use this chapter to orient your own on-going research and awareness, as the picture changes!

Your objectives

In this chapter you will learn about the following.

(a) The context influencing government approaches to training and development

(b) The competency movement and the development of NVQs

(c) The role of the Qualifications and Curriculum Authority (QCA)

(d) The role of Learning and Skills Councils (LSC)

(e) Specific general and vocational training initiatives, including: modern apprenticeships, Investors in People, New Deal and the University for Industry

(f) The role of Union Learning Representatives in employee development

1 SKILLS AND EMPLOYMENT IN THE UK

1.1 Vocational education and training in the UK

Research over some decades has highlighted poor levels of organisational investment in education and training in the UK, compared to its key competitors (Constable and McCormick, 1987; National Skills Task Force, 1998). Bolton (1997) summarises the position as follows.

> Study after study... has repeated the assertion that at the top end of training and education, the United Kingdom does as well as any other nation with, for instance, the proportion of young people achieving university degrees. It is at the intermediate level of qualification, the technician, the apprenticeship, secretarial and clerical training, that we do so poorly. It is generally recognised that the UK trains about half the number of young people with these skills as do many of our competitors.

This has been attributed to a number of factors.

(a) Entrenched philosophies of organisation and management which maximise managerial control through the micro-design of jobs, automation and close supervision. Such systems devalue the role of employee development, other than at a basic competence level.

(b) The emergence of human capital theory, which views HRD as an investment. While positive in supporting a business case for HRD, this viewpoint may cause a narrow focus on return on investment (direct contribution to profits). Development activities with less quantifiable or longer-term benefits may be seen as a cost to be minimised or cut, particularly in the face of competition for scarce resources, pressures to meet short-term financial targets and global economic recession.

(c) Lack of systematic human resource planning, in the face of changing labour markets, so that skill requirements and shortages are not identified as an impetus to HRD.

(d) A voluntarist or market-led approach to skill development, whereby responsibility for HRD decisions and funding lies primarily with employers, rather than with government. Many employers will choose to minimise their investment in training, where demand for skills is not perceived to be pressing.

(e) Self-limitation to low-skilled product and service markets. The deputy director of SKOPE (Skills, Knowledge and Organisational Performance) has been quoted as saying: 'Employers can happily ignore the government's warning about the effects of globalisation. In today's climate many firms can and do compete successfully on low skills and by producing goods at the low end of product specialisation. There is no impetus for them to change.'

(Manocha, 2003)

FOR DISCUSSION

Why do you think UK employers have been so reluctant to develop their people?

INTERNATIONAL COMPARISONS

	UK	Germany	US	Japan
Extent of State intervention	Voluntarist (left to employers)	Directed (laws and guidelines require employers to provide training funding and resources)	Voluntarist (anti-federalist, with wide variation)	Voluntarist/directed (voluntary, provision, but strong directives setting and enforcing high-quality training standards)
Orientation to development	Finance (rather than industry) oriented. Individualist development. Development largely extraneous to corporate culture: seen in context of performance improvement or management succession	Industry oriented (eg engineering) Functionally specific	Individualist: trainee aspirations, effort, reward. Excellent training by leading companies – otherwise unco-ordinated.	Collectivist view of development. On-going long-term training within employment: structured development for individual/organis-ation benefit. Development embedded in corporate culture, open to all employees

In the 1980s, recognition of the UK's poor skill base in relation to global competitors, supported by growing business/employer influence, led policy makers and educationalists to seek ways to shift the emphasis in education towards **vocational skills**. Competence approaches (aimed at defining, developing and assessing competent performance of specific job-related tasks) were introduced along side other aspects of change in education – including the National Curriculum, GCSEs, General National Vocational Qualifications (GNVQs) and the use of problem-based and experiential learning – which focus on learners' development of skills and abilities, rather than on purely theoretical knowledge.

The 1990s saw the development of a broader agenda, responding to the challenges of global competition, developments in ICT and the transition from manufacturing to service- and knowledge-based economies. The Department for Education and Employment – and its successor, the Department for Education and Skills – engaged in intensive research, strategy and standard development. (The Department for Business, Innovation and Skills – BIS – now has responsibility for further and higher education and skills, as of June 2009. The Department for Children, Schools and Families – DCSF – is responsible for education of people aged 14-19.)

A Skills Task Force was set up in 1998 to develop a National Skills Agenda to 'ensure that Britain has the skills needed to sustain high levels of employment, compete in the global marketplace and provide opportunity for all' (National Skills Task Force, 1998). The Task Force conducted a series of major research reports, case studies and skills surveys which revealed a number of issues.

(a) Mismatch between skill supply and demand (notably in technical jobs)

(b) Lack of systematic analysis of future skill requirements

(c) Lack of training for lower-level and flexible workers, particularly in small organisations

(d) Lack of qualified adults in the workforce, especially compared with major European competitors such as France and Germany.

The Government's 2003 White Paper *21st Century Skills: Realising Our Potential* argued that despite extensive intervention, the UK still had gaps in basic skills (including literacy, numeracy and ICT); intermediate skills (such as at professional, apprenticeship and technician level) and higher-level leadership and management skills.

EXAMPLE

The National Employers Skills Survey 2007

Over 79,000 employers in different sectors and localities in England took part in the latest National Employers Skills Survey (NESS), commissioned by the LSC, in collaboration with the (then) Department for Innovation, Universities and Skills (DIUS) and the Sector Skills Development Agency (SSDA).

Among their key findings were the following.

- 67% of employers have funded or arranged training in the last year
- Employer training spend for 2007 was £38.6bn, an increase of 16%
- Almost half of employers have a training plan and over a third have a training budget
- There was a reduction on the number of vacancies caused by a lack of skills (21%, compared to 25% in 2005)

- Over all, there has been a steady upward trend in most areas of recruitment, skills gaps and training

(Learning and Skills Council, May 2008)

For more details, go to:
http://research.lsc.gov.uk/LSC+Research/publisehd/ness/ness2007

1.2 Skills, employment and competitiveness

Low training and skill levels raised concerns about *national economic performance*, due to:

(a) The potential inability of many UK firms to respond to changing world economic conditions and technological developments

(b) Poor productivity and competitiveness compared with other countries

(c) Self-limitation to competing in relatively low-skilled product and service markets

(d) The social costs of having a rising proportion of the potential labour force condemned to long-term economic inactivity because of inadequate skills (including literacy and numeracy).

Bratton and Gold (2007) note that the economic case for investment in human resource development can be made at different levels.

(a) At the individual level, there is a close relationships between learning (in various forms) and job prospects, especially in terms of minimising unemployment and increasing overall earnings.

(b) At the organisational level, HRD is a central feature of a 'bundle' of HRM practices which have been shown to impact on corporate performance. HRD itself may offer measurable financial returns on investment – and may also contribute less readily quantifiable benefits, such as employee commitment and organisational flexibility.

(c) At the level of the national economy and society as a whole, there is a demonstrable connection between school enrolments, the proportion of the labour force in higher education and the level and growth of the nation's gross domestic product (GDP). Skill levels are argued to be important for future national competitiveness. Low qualifications also prevent entry into the labour market and contribute to the emerging problems of **social exclusion**. *Bridging the Gap*, the 1999 Social Exclusion Unit Report, found that 9% of 16-18 year olds were not in education, training or work, creating a mix of educational, health and social welfare problems. This has become a key focus of government policy-making in recent years.

Activity 1 **(20 minutes)**

'Michael Porter, in his recent DTI-sponsored review of UK competitiveness, said that labour force skills continue to be an area of competitive disadvantage for the UK. It has been estimated that poor skills levels account for up to a fifth of the productivity gap. All of which provides compelling support for the official line that the country needs to upskill to boost the economy.

'But do raised skill levels directly equate to increased productivity?' (Manocha, 2003)

From our discussion in this and the previous chapter, suggest two reasons why raising skill *levels* might not directly equate to increased *productivity*.

1.3 Government policy on training and development

Interventionist approaches to HRD seek to influence organisational decision-making in the interests of the economy as a whole. In France, for example, there is a highly-developed concept of 'social partnership' between government and organisations, supported by tax levies on organisations to fund training grants.

Under the UK's voluntarist approach, the role of government (and related agencies) is seen primarily as encouraging and facilitating organisational training.

(a) **Stimulating employer demand** for skills and investment in education and training: researching and promoting the business case for learning and development, and promoting benchmark HRD standards such as Investors in People (discussed in Section 3 below).

(b) **Developing the national training infrastructure**, including:

  (i) The establishment of an integrated **framework of vocational qualifications** based on national standards: National Vocational Qualifications (NVQs) in England and Wales, and SVQs (Scottish Vocational Qualifications) in Scotland (discussed in Section 2 of this chapter)

  (ii) The establishment of a national **network of regionally-based institutions** to co-ordinate, finance and administer delivery of national training programmes. This was previously the role of Training and Enterprise Councils (TECs) and Local Enterprise Councils (LECs) in Scotland. The regional basis of the network allowed links with local authorities and chambers of commerce, careers services in schools, local Job Centres and so on, fostering business support and community awareness. In the interests of greater clarity and co-ordination, these were replaced in 2001 by the Learning Skills Council (LSC) and its local delivery units (discussed in Section 3 of this chapter) and later the Young People's Learning Agency and the Skills Funding Agency.

(c) **Providing funding for specific initiatives to support HRD**, where the market alone fails to maintain sufficient levels of demand and investment. A number of national initiatives are aimed at enhancing the employability of young people and their access to training, including New Deal (formerly Youth Training) and Connexions (discussed in Section 3 of this chapter.)

(d) Stimulating **demand for learning**. The Green Paper, *The Learning Age: a Renaissance for a New Britain* (DfEE, 1998) set out the government's vision for '**lifelong learning**' and the '**learning society**'. A key policy goal of the Lifelong Learning agenda is to drive up the demand for learning, of any kind, among individuals. The theory is that if individuals can be encouraged to engage in learning activities, this will improve their employability *and* their openness to further learning within organisations, creating the impetus for continuous improvement that is a key to competitive advantage. This particularly applies to unqualified adults who have previously been excluded from the training market. Initiatives launched to support individual education and learning include the University for Industry (UfI) and learndirect (discussed in Section 3 below).

Further and higher education and skilling are, as of June 2009, within the remit of a new Department for Business, Innovation and Skills (BIS) – a merger of the former BERR (Department for Business, Enterprise and Regulatory Reform) and DIUS (Department for Innovation, Universities and Skills): watch the news for new initiatives, name changes and new website development!

Activity 2 **(5 minutes)**

What sources of information can you monitor regularly, in order to keep up to date with government policy on skills, training, life-long learning and other aspects of HRD?

We will now look at some of the key areas of training infrastructure discussed above, starting with the development of competence-based training.

2 COMPETENCE-BASED TRAINING

2.1 The competence movement

Historically, the UK has shown an educational bias towards knowledge – and educational institutions and occupations which deal in knowledge – rather than practical skills. The poor performance of British industry and management (as discussed earlier) provided political impetus towards the definition and development of more practical, demonstrable workplace competences.

> The concept of training for competence is that it should be criterion related, directed at developing the ability of trainees to perform specific tasks directly related to the job they are in, or for which they are preparing, expressed in terms of performance outcomes and specific indicators. It is a reaction against the confetti-scattering approach to training as being a good thing in its own right, concerned with the general education of people dealing with general matters. (Torrington *et al*, 2002)

The idea has been around for some time, having its roots in teacher education in the US, but only gained currency in the UK in the 1980s. The Review of Vocational Qualifications in England and Wales (RVQ) Working Group report in April 1986 recommended the introduction of NVQs, to address weaknesses in the then current system, including (www.qca.org.uk/TheStoryOfNVQ):

- Assessment methods biased towards testing of knowledge rather than skill or competence
- Insufficient recognition of learning gained outside formal education and training
- Many barriers to accessing vocational qualifications and inadequate arrangements for progression and transfer of credit
- Limited take-up of vocational qualifications.

The National Council for Vocational Qualifications (NCVQ) – subsequently the Qualification and Curriculum Authority (QCA), and now the Qualification and Curriculum Development Agency (QCDA) – was formed to develop criteria for a clear, coherent and comprehensive system of vocational qualifications. This led to National Vocational Qualifications (NVQs, discussed below) and a wide range of other vocational qualifications (VQs) accredited within the framework.

Competence-based training and assessment has been enthusiastically promoted by the government, proponents of management development (such as the Management Charter Initiative) and professional bodies, as a way of:

(a) Supporting the career and development aspirations of learners without the historical bias towards formal academic achievement: NVQs, for example, have no formal pre-entry qualifications

(b) Supporting flexible and job-relevant learning, through on-going training and assessment in the workplace, with no pre-determined time-frame for completion, and potentially minimal inputs from education providers

(c) Supporting employers' objectives for HRD, by focusing on relevant job skills. Competence frameworks and assessments also support a range of HR planning and performance management applications

(d) Supporting employees' employability objectives. NVQs, for example, are modularised, so that learning can be transferred freely between providers and elements can be tackled in any order (to suit job- and employer-related priorities).

2.2 Government qualifications agencies

The Qualifications and Curriculum Authority (QCA) (ACCAC in Wales and SQA in Scotland) developed the National Qualification Framework, which creates a coherent classification for NVQs. It was the regulatory authority in charge of the formal recognition of all standards and qualifications in education and training, including the National Curriculum, GNVQs, NVQs and technical certificates awarded under Modern Apprenticeship schemes, but excluding university degrees, which are dealt with by the Quality Assurance Agency..

In 2007, the government decided to set up **Ofqual** as an independent exams regulator. Ofqual has now taken over the QCA'a regulatory role. The QCA was left with the role of developing of qualifications, syllabuses and assessments and is now known as the **Qualifications and Curriculum Development Authority**, (QCDA).

2.3 National Vocational Qualifications (NVQs)

NVQs and SVQs are part of the National Qualifications Framework in the UK. They are work-related, competence-based qualifications, reflecting the skills and knowledge needed to do a job effectively.

'NVQs are based on **national occupational standards**: statements of performance that describe what competent people in a particular occupation are expected to be able to do. They cover all the main aspects of an occupation, including current best practice, the ability to adapt to future requirements and the knowledge and understanding that underpin competent performance' (www.qca.org.uk).

Competence frameworks are **developed** by *Sector Bodies* (previously Standards Setting Bodies) new sector skills councils (ssc), overseen by the Sector Skills Development Agency (SSDA). Qualifications are **delivered** through a network of training centres (eg local colleges) which are approved by one of several **awarding bodies** (eg EdExcel, City and Guilds and professional bodies) which in turn must be **accredited** by the QCDA (or its equivalents).

Standards of competence identify the key roles of a given occupation and break them down into areas or units of competence. These in turn are formulated as statements describing what a competent person should be able to do at different levels, including:

- The specific activities concerned (elements of competence)
- To what standard (performance criteria)
- In what contexts and conditions (listed in a range statement)
- With what underpinning knowledge and understanding.

Activity 3 **(30 minutes)**

Use your existing knowledge (eg of the HNC/HND qualification) or research skills to find out how the five levels of competence for NVQs are defined.

Torrington *et al* (2002) note that NVQs have had a 'rough ride' since the concept was first introduced. There have been reservations in relation to:

(a) **Standards**. Employers inevitably care more about fulfilling their own skill requirements then those of the national employment base – and may find occupational standards too general and/or over-onerous for their own needs. In some areas – such as management – competence frameworks inevitably oversimplify the complexity and need for flexibility of the work.

(b) **Assessment**. The assessment process is time-consuming, particularly in view of the bureaucracy (and specialist terminology) involved. The need to collect acceptable evidence of competence may distract attention from learning, work requirements and other development needs. The quality of assessment also depends heavily on individual assessors: there has been some pressure to re-introduce written examinations in some settings.

(c) **Educational issues**. Since the training agenda is set by the demonstration of job performance, there may be a lack (and future loss) of training in cognitive (thinking) skills. The framework does not address the difficulties of defining higher-level competencies (eg creative conceptual skills) or underlying issues such as the reluctance of UK employers to invest in training.

However, NVQs and SVQs have certainly added to the number of vocational qualifications offered and attained in the UK. They are also (as we noted earlier) an important part of the national infrastructure and the basis of training targets.

2.4 The Management Charter Initiative

The MCI was set up in 1988, as the operating arm of the National Forum for Management Education and Development. Its aims were to:

(a) Define generic standards of assessment for management competence

(b) Promote 'best practice' in management education, training and development

(c) Develop ethical and qualification standards with a view to the eventual 'professionalising' of management under a chartered body.

Managerial qualifications were originally developed by the MCI, as the basis for NVQs and SVQs in Management and Team Leading. However, the **Management Standards Centre** took over the work of developing and championing a new set of National Occupational Standards (NOS) for management and leadership, launched in 2005, and revised in 2008. It is currently the government-recognised standards setting body in this area.

The 2008 Standards cover six functional areas within the management and leadership fields.

A Managing Self and Personal Skills
B Proving Direction
C Facilitating Change
D Working with People
E Using Resources, and
F Achieving Results.

Each function has a list of Units of Competence, which combined in a modular approach lead to:

- Level 2 NVQ/SVQ in Team Leading
- Levels 3, 4 or 5 NVQ/SVQ in Management (depending on different levels at which the functions are exercised)

Weblink

The full 2008 Standards can be downloaded from the Management Standards Centre.

►► **http://www.management-standards.org**

The competence-based approach to management development appears to have taken hold in the UK. Some observers, however, note that organisations are beginning to move away from the standard model and towards:

(a) **In-house frameworks**, reflecting specific organisational culture and context

(b) The use of more '**holistic**' forms of development, underpinning specific competences with a wider skill base, employability training, mentoring, self-managed and experiential learning, learning to learn and so on.

FOR DISCUSSION

How far can managerial work be defined or assessed as competences? For which particular aspects of a manager's job would it be hard to demonstrate 'outputs'? What other approaches to management qualifications would you propose?

---

3 CONTEMPORARY TRAINING INITIATIVES

3.1 Learning and Skills Council

The **Learning and Skills Council** was set up in April 2001, bringing various learning providers together under a single funding regime. It was responsible for funding and planning all education and training for over 16-year-olds in England, other than in universities. It has been succeeded by the Young People's Learning Agency and the Skills Funding Agency.

(a) The **Young People's Learning Agency** supports the delivery of education and training to young people in England. It provides:

- Financial support for young learners
- Funding for Academies
- Support for local government commissioning of education and training

(b) The **Skills Funding Agency** funds and regulates adult further education and skills training in England.

3.2 Train To Gain

Train to Gain is a service linking employers with an experienced **Skills Broker** (trained by the LSC) whose role is to offer impartial and independent advice to businesses; match identified training needs with appropriate training providers; and ensure that training is delivered to meet business needs. According to the programme's website: 'This marks a cultural shift in how skills training will be delivered, and will ensure that the delivery of training is much more flexible and responds to business needs.' (www.traintogain.gov.uk)

Skills Brokers:

- Help employers to identify skilling needs in response to business goals and constraints
- Make recommendations based on the skills analysis in order to help businesses pinpoint the types of training required, appropriate providers, qualification schemes and so on
- Agree a training package with the employer and selected training provider

- Recommend funding options or provide access to funding (eg wage compensation for firms with fewer than 50 employees)
- Provide support and progress review as the training package is delivered.

Train To Gain also funds training initiated under the **Skills Pledge**. The pledge, recommended by the 2006 Leitch Review of Skills, is a voluntary commitment by firms to help staff develop basic literacy and numeracy skills and work towards Level 2 qualifications. Arriva, EDF Energy and First Group were among early signatories along with all central government departments.

3.3 Apprenticeships

The UK government launched 'Modern Apprenticeship' in 1994 in an attempt to involve industry more closely in the process of vocational training. Apprenticeships (traditionally available in crafts and engineering sectors) are available in childcare, tourism, travel, retail and a range of other industries.

The apprenticeship model combines vocational education (towards NVQ Level 3) including core skills development (literacy, numeracy, communication and so on) with hands-on experience in a sponsoring organisation. Apprentices are attached to a particular employer for the purposes of training: there is no guarantee of employment at the end of the training period.

Apprenticeships are now administered by National Apprenticeship Service, which works with employers (via Business Link and the Department of Children, Schools and Families (DCSF) to promote, fund and co-ordinate apprenticeships throughout England.

FOR DISCUSSION

The Adult Learning Inspectorate (ALI) failed 46% of work-based training schemes in inspections throughout 2002/2003, although this was an improvement on the year before (www.ali.gov.uk). The Association of Learning Providers countered that judgements on performance were made on incorrectly defined measures: for example, a person leaving a modern apprenticeship for a better paid, better skilled job constituted a 'failure'.

What do you think is a 'successful' outcome for an Apprenticeship, for all the stakeholders concerned?

3.4 Investors in People

The Investors in People scheme (IiP) was launched in 1991 by the National Training Taskforce, together with the Confederation of British Industry (CBI), Trades Union Congress (TUC), the Institute of Personnel and Development (IPD) (now the CIPD) and leading national businesses. It was designed to provide a national benchmark standard for investment in employee training and development. IiP is delivered in the UK by local Learning and Skills Councils and 'Business Links' (the Small Business Service), which have targets for the number of organisations committing to the scheme and attaining the standard.

Organisations seeking accreditation must audit their current training practice and provision (with the aid of survey instruments provided) and bring them into line with published standards. They are required to produce evidence of their training objectives and standards, which are assessed by the LSC. The programme is not intended to be a prescriptive set of rules and procedures: organisations are encouraged to develop their own solutions and methods towards benchmark standards. The key principles are set out on the IiP website.

(a) **Commitment** to invest in people to achieve business goals

(b) **Planning** how skills, individuals and teams are to be developed to achieve these goals

(c) **Action** to develop and use necessary skills in a well defined and continuing programme directly tied to business objectives

(d) **Evaluating** outcomes of training and development for individuals' progress towards goals, the value achieved and future needs.

Commitment to IiP requires significant time, effort and investment – potentially including major cultural change. The benefits of IiP status have been debated. Some studies have shown an increase in commitment to HR development, a belief in the value of the process and perceived performance gains, particularly where it was used to assess performance and implement continuous improvement (Alberga *et al*, 1997). The IiP website devotes a whole page to the standard's benefits, and a library of successful case studies.

EXAMPLE

'Although the Pontin's name is well known to British holiday makers, the Pontin's of the 21st century is very different from the traditional "holiday camp" of the past. New managing director Colin Homer is turning a loss-making organisation into a profitable one, using Investors in People to improve the core area of the business... namely its employees.

'This is a human resources challenge most managers would baulk at: 300 full-time employees are joined each Spring by 1,600 seasonal workers whose turnover has meant that, in past years, Pontin's has had to employ over 5,000 people during the summer season to fill the 1,600 positions... But as a staunch advocate of the business benefits that Investors in People recognition brings, Colin Homer is already seeing improved employee retention – which will in turn result in greater productivity and reduced costs.

'Pontin's can now give employees more and better reasons for staying with the company... Following the guidance of Investors in People, Pontin's is now putting in place a structure whereby every employee will have:

- a personal development file with job descriptions and aims
- access to NVQs
- access to funding for vocational training
- assistance with professional qualifications
- assessment of aims and goals and help in achieving them.

'Even if someone only stays for a matter of months, they should still have a new qualification to take to their next job.

(Investors in People, 2004)

Some organisations, however, have struggled to find real benefits through the process.

(a) There can be difficulties administering the process.

(b) It encourages organisations to underrate the importance of informal development methods.

(c) It does not imply genuine commitment to improving development, since organisations may seek IiP status purely as a rubber stamp for their employer brand.

(d) It is a 'spurious' tool for stimulating the demand for organisational HRD, because many of the organisations achieving the standard were already convinced of its benefits and doing what was required (Bratton and Gold, 2007).

Activity 4 **(no time limit)**

Check out the Investors in People website (www.investorsinpeople.co.uk) and view the Investors in People Standard itself. Use it as a checklist to do a quick appraisal of your own organisation: would it (broadly) qualify as an 'Investor in People'? What areas would have to be brought in line with the Standard?

3.5 New Deal

New Deal is delivered by Jobcentre Plus, through its network of Jobcentres. It is a key part of the Government's strategy to:

(a) Get people off benefits and into work, giving long-term unemployed people the opportunity to develop or upgrade their skills

(b) Improve the overall skills base and employability of the UK workforce.

The **New Deal for Young People** programme is mandatory for jobseekers aged 18 to 24 who have been unemployed for 6 months or more and are claiming Jobseeker's Allowance. The initial part of the programme is a concentrated period of help and advice in order to help them to find work. The government offers subsidies to employers who take on a full-time or part-time New Deal employee, plus a grant towards certified vocational training. Candidates become employees under normal terms and conditions, and training arrangements must be agreed with a New Deal personal adviser.

The **New Deal 25 Plus** programme is also mandatory for those claiming Jobseeker's Allowance for 18 months or more. Jobseekers undertake short courses to refresh existing skills or learn new skills. Employers are given the option of taking candidates on Work Trial. They are also offered subsidies to take candidates on for six months, full-time or part-time, allowing long-term unemployed people to gain work experience and show what they can do.

There are also a number of voluntary programmes, including:

(a) **New Deal for Lone Parents**: advice on childcare, access to training and help with applications for in-work benefits.

(b) **New Deal 50 Plus**: advice and assistance with job search, and access to retraining.

(c) **New Deal for Disabled People**: advice and support from Job Brokers, who can also work with employers to adapt the workplace for disabled people.

The new sector-specific **Ambition Programme** works with business leaders in sectors with skills shortages that would not ordinarily recruit jobless people (IT, retail, construction and energy) to:

(a) Improve placement and retention rates of New Deal participants in jobs with good career potential, not usually accessible to unemployed people

(b) Meet employer HR and skill shortages.

Employers' hiring requirements are used to define training needs and standards of job readiness of New Deal candidates, with a steering group of business leaders from each sector overseeing the programme.

Activity 5 **(5 minutes)**

What would be the potential benefits to employers of taking on people who join New Deal 25 Plus, voluntary programmes or Ambition Programme?

3.6 University for Industry and learndirect

Ufi Ltd is one of the Government's key partners in delivering its workforce development and lifelong learning agendas. It 'aims to drive up demand for learning, help adults improve their employability by acquiring new knowledge and skills, and help businesses become more competitive' (www.ufi.com).

Ufi works with a broad range of public and private providers in local, employer and sector-based 'hubs', to deliver mainly online courses and information through a network of e-learning centres. One of its priorities is meeting the training needs of small and medium-sized enterprises (SMEs), although it also works with many large employers, including Barclays, Nissan, Tesco and Remploy. Ufi also works with the Skills for Life Strategy Unit (formerly the Adult Basic Skills Strategy Unit) and awarding bodies to offer National Certificates in Adult Literacy and Numeracy, through online tests. Additional links with further and higher education establishments should develop more e-learning routes to accredited qualifications, while a pilot scheme is currently working with 14 – 16 year olds who have been excluded from mainstream schooling.

As the world's largest supported e-learning network, Ufi plays a key part in delivering the government's e-learning strategy (*Towards a Unified e-Learning*, July 2003): 'E-learning should become a standard feature of learning and teaching for all ages, from school children to pensioners, throughout the education system, in the workplace and beyond.' (Ufi, 2003).

learndirect is a government-sponsored network of online learning and information services, developed by Ufi in 2000 to help deliver workforce development and lifelong learning. In particular, it aims to support the government's vision of a 'learning society' where people can access learning opportunities and upgrade their skills throughout their lives, whether they are: employees seeking to improve their workplace skills; job seekers wishing to improve their employability; people who feel excluded from the world of education or IT; or just interest learners.

learndirect offers supported flexible learning courses in three main categories: skills for life (literacy, numeracy and ESOL); business and management; and IT skills. Over 80% of courses are online, while others are delivered via workbooks or CD-ROM.

learndirect's free information and advice service (delivered by phone helpline and web site) offers guidance to adults wanting to access learning opportunities.

learndirect can be accessed via over 2,000 e-learning centres located throughout England, Wales and Northern Ireland in high street locations, libraries colleges and workplaces. There are also 'virtual learning centres' run completely online, allowing enrolment and learning from home, libraries or wherever users wish.

Activity 6 **(no time limit)**

Check out the learndirect website at:

www.learndirect.co.uk

How might you use learndirect as part of your own self-managed learning? How might you use it to develop Human Resources?

3.7 Connexions

Connexions is the government's support service for young people aged 13-19 in England, joining up the work of six government Departments and their agencies, together with private and voluntary sector groups and youth and careers services.

Launched in April 2003, it offers practical help with choosing and accessing courses and careers – as well as personal counselling on issues like drug abuse and homelessness. Connexions was initially delivered through local Partnerships – based on LSC areas, working to national planning guidelines and managed and monitored by local management committees. From April 2008, however, funding and delivery was transferred to Local Authorities (*Education and Skills Act 2008*), under the Department for Children, Schools and Families. It is also delivered on-line, via Connexions Direct.

'Connexions is the government's ambitious attempt to stop young people bouncing from pillar to post for support during their transition to adulthood. The previous services geared towards young people formed a patchwork of provision, with too many teenagers falling through the gaps and joining the drop-out generation' (Prasad, 2003).

Personal advisers are deployed in schools, colleges and the community, available on an outreach basis to provide support and guidance on formulating goals and accessing relevant services.

FOR DISCUSSION

How is Connexions relevant to employers?

3.8 National Skills Academies

'National Skills Academies are employer-led centres of training excellence. The government's mission is to create a world class workforce by delivering the skills that employers need in each sector of the economy.

Skills Academies take different shapes and forms, ranging from purpose-built training centres to online courses tailored to the needs of each sector.

Crucially, skills academies are led by employers who work with government and training providers to shape the training and qualifications that will help them compete in global markets.'

(http://www.nationalskillsacademy.co.uk/about/index.html, recovered 22 August 2010)

3.9 Sector Skills Councils

Sector Skills Councils are government sponsored but employer led organisations. Each Council deals with a separate sector of the economy. Their goals in training are to improve individual skill levels and to reduce skill shortages. They contribute to the development of National Occupational Standards, apprenticeship frameworks, sector skills agreements and sector qualification strategies. They are supervised by the UK Commission for Employment and Skills, which, together with the Alliance of Sector Skills Councils, has replaced the Sector Skills and Development Agency.

3.10 Union Learning Representatives

Increasing employee demand for training and development is a feature of the new psychological contract of employment. Trade unions have for some years worked for the development of their members, developing learning provision and creating demand from sections of the workforce that had little access to employer-provided training: manual workers, part-timers, older and ethnic minority workers and so on.

In 1998, the TUC set up a task group to examine how to improve the role of trade unions in learning. It proposed a network of Union Learning Representatives (ULRs) in workplaces to: analyse members' training needs; provide members with information and advice on learning matters; arrange learning and training and promote its value to members; and consult with the employer on union members' learning and training. The Union Learning Fund provides training for ULRs and contributes to the costs of developing and co-ordinating learning programmes.

The government has supported ULRs as important contributors to its basic skills, social inclusion and lifelong learning agendas. The network has grown rapidly: the TUC hoped to have 22,000 reps in place by 2010. The *Employment Protection Act 2002* awarded ULRs paid time off for reps to perform their duties.

The benefit of having union learning representatives (ULRs) in the workplace are said to be as follows.

(a) They are a trained and inexpensive source of training advice for employers.

(b) They are trusted by, and have access to, workers who might not otherwise engage in learning. This contributes to equal opportunities and inclusion, 'reaching out in particular to people who do not do well in formal education or who need help with English as a second language' (Margolis, 2003).

(c) They support learning focused on the employees' development needs – not just immediate job training – and this has benefits to employers, through increased openness to learning, continuous improvement, confidence, improvement in basic skills, employability and so on.

(d) They are advocates for training, ensuring that line managers follow through with agreed time off, resources and so on, against pressures to side-line development activities.

EXAMPLE

Although the law does not provide for paid time off for workers to study, ACAS reckons that some companies are already doing this. One example is Sainsbury's, which has encouraged the ULR initiative and allows learning to happen in working time.

It all started in 2001, when a deputy shop steward made an approach to the company to introduce a lifelong learning project. He devised a plan that involved sending learner reps on a 10-day course promoting basic skills awareness. In April 2002, a successful bid was made to the LSC for £100,000 of funding for courses in Sainsbury's depots in Hertfordshire... Sainsbury's now has 73 learner reps. The project has grown so fast that there is a rep in each region... ULRs deliver courses when they are needed to suit shift work. 'In a climate of multi-racial employment, we found huge demand for courses in English as a second language, in particular', [Sarah Lacey, learning rep for the Union of Shop, Distributive and Allied Workers] explains. 'Sainsbury's has done a marvellous job in recognising a basic skills need and allows two hours paid time off a week', she says. 'People do not have to give up their own time to attend. For the company, the benefits have been phenomenal too.'

(Margolis, 2003)

FOR DISCUSSION

What does the example above suggest about the impact of HRD on employee relations?

Chapter roundup

- Vocational education and training in the UK has traditionally suffered from low levels of employer commitment and investment, leading to skill gaps, lack of competitiveness and social exclusion of people lacking basic skills.
- Government policy on VET has focused on: stimulating employer demand for skills; developing the national qualifications framework (including NVQs); establishing regionally-based institutions to deliver training programmes; initiatives for employability training; and stimulating a demand for life-long learning and basic skill development.
- The competency movement has supported training for competence as a way of focusing attention on transferable, employable, competitive vocational skills. NVQs are based on national occupation standards. Management competencies were first developed by the Management Charter Initiative.
- The Learning and Skills Council has been superseded by the Young People's hearing Agency and Skills Funding Agency with responsibility for planning and funding all education and training for over-16 year olds in England, other than in universities. The Qualifications and Curriculum Agency is responsible for the formal recognition of all standards and qualifications in education and training.
- A range of training initiatives has been launched to involve industry in education and training (Modern Apprenticeships); define benchmark standards in HRD (Investors in People); improve the employability of unemployed people (New Deal); encourage lifelong, flexible and e-learning (Ufl/learndirect); and support young people in accessing learning (Connexions) often through employer-led programmes (National Skills Academies and Sector Skills Councils).
- Union Learning Representatives contribute to the basic skills, social inclusion and lifelong learning agendas by supporting workplace learning.

Quick quiz

1 What are some of the causes of poor investment in training in the UK?

2 What is the theory behind the Lifelong Learning Agenda?

3 What are the advantages and disadvantages of NVQs?

4 What do QCDA, MCI and liP stand for?

5 An Advanced Modern Apprenticeship includes a Level 2 NVQ component. True or false?

6 What are the four principles of Investors in People?

7 Which government programme is mandatory for a 24-year old who has been unemployed for six months or more and is claiming Jobseeker's Allowance?

8 The world's largest supported e-learning network is:

   A Connexions
   B Ufl
   C SVQ
   D The Ambition Programme

9 What are the advantages of having Union learning representatives in the workplace?

Answers to quick quiz

1 Philosophies of organisation and management; human capital theory; lack of HRP; voluntarist framework; self limitation to low-skill markets

2 Encouraging individuals to engage in learning of any kind improves their employability and openness to learning, creating a culture of continuous improvement.

3 See paragraphs 2.1 and 2.3 for a full answer.

4 Qualifications and Curriculum Development Authority; Management Charter Initiative; Investors in People

5 False: Level 3.

6 Commitment, planning, action, evaluation

7 New Deal for Young people

8 B

9 See paragraph 3.8 for a full answer

Answers to activities

1 Manocha himself identifies two problems with the more-training-equals-higher-productivity equation.

(a) 'The UK doesn't simply need higher-level skills: it needs the *right* skills. As many a dinner party conversation has recorded, while the UK pushes for more graduates, we are short of plumbers...' The government is addressing this by matching skills output with industry requirements (as we see later in the chapter).

(b) 'What happens to the higher-skilled people? Many commentators point out that the productivity gap will not be closed by training people and then sending them back to an unreceptive workplace, where new skills are wasted through lack of opportunity.' We noted the need for transfer of learning in Chapter 1.

2 Suggestions include: quality national press; HRM and HRD journals; websites of relevant organisations (starting with the Department of Education & Skills).

3 As set out at www.dfes.gov.uk/nvq/what (although you could have used a number of other information sources), the five levels are as follows.

Level 1 Competence which involves the application of knowledge in the performance of a range of varied work activities, most of which may be routine and predictable

Level 2 Competence which involves the application of knowledge in a significant range of varied work activities, performed in a variety of context. Some of these activities are complex or non-routine and there is some individual responsibility or autonomy. Collaboration with others, perhaps through membership of a work group or team, may often be a requirement.

Level 3 Competence which involves the application of knowledge in a broad range of varied work activities performed in a wide variety of contexts, most of which are complex and non-routine. There is considerable responsibility and autonomy and control or guidance of others is often required.

Level 4 Competence which involves the application of knowledge in a broad range of complex, technical or professional work activities performed in a variety of contexts and with a substantial degree of personal responsibility and autonomy. Responsibility for the work of others and the allocations of resources is often present.

Level 5 Competence which involves the application of a range of fundamental principles across a wide and often unpredictable variety of contexts. Very substantial personal autonomy and often significant responsibility for the work of others and for the allocation of substantial resources feature strongly, as do personal accountabilities for analysis, diagnosis, design, planning, execution and evaluation.

4 Your own research and application.

5 The key benefit to employers is ease of access to potential employees who may already have the skills and experience required, and who have had guidance in training to meet employer requirements (especially in the Ambition programme). In the case of voluntary programmes, it may also support equal opportunity programmes. The financial incentives should not be the primary benefit – but may help to reduce the risk.

6 Your own research. If you had trouble accessing the information, what does this say about the programme?

Part B

Employee Relations

Chapter 4:

THE CONTEXT OF EMPLOYEE RELATIONS

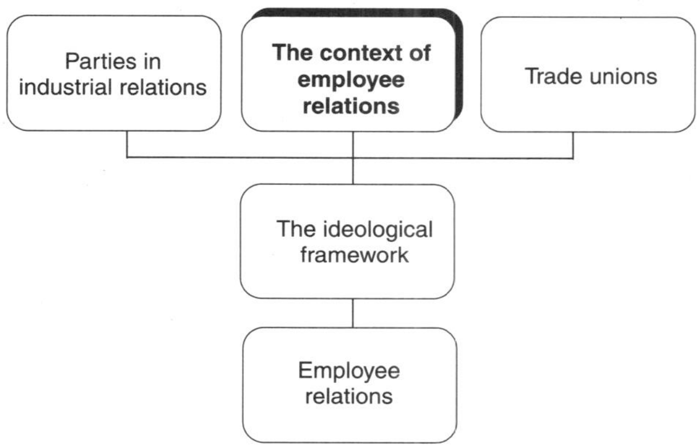

Introduction

Thanks largely to its turbulent history and tainting with political colours, industrial relations is an emotive subject which requires careful handling in study and professional contexts: as you read, try to appreciate both sides of the debate.

Traditionally, **industrial relations** are the dealings and co-operation (or lack of it) between management and workers, usually via their representatives in a trade union or staff association. However, trade unionism has been on the decline in the UK (and USA) and a high proportion of employees do not now belong to unions. Nevertheless, industrial relations still exist in organisations. A shift to the term '**employee relations**' reflects a broader orientation towards communication with and involvement of employees, and a more unitarist perspective in which co-operation is regarded as both possible and desirable in order for business' and employees' needs to be met.

In this chapter we will consider the players and ideologies involved in industrial relations and the shift towards 'employee relations'. In Chapters 5 and 6 we will examine more closely some of the processes involved in the management of employee relations.

Your objectives

In this chapter you will learn about the following.

(a) The unitary and pluralistic frames of reference
(b) The development of trade unions and the nature of industrial relations
(c) The role of a trade union and its contribution to effective industrial relations
(d) The ideological framework of industrial relations
(e) Distinguish between industrial relations and employee relations
(f) The roles taken by the main actors in employee relations
(g) The impact of human resource management on employee relations

1 PARTIES IN INDUSTRIAL RELATIONS

1.1 What are industrial relations?

Definition

Industrial relations (IR) comprises 'all the rules, practices and conventions governing interactions between managements and their workforces, normally involving collective employee representation and bargaining.'

(Graham and Bennett, 1998)

Industrial relations policy and practice covers a number of areas.

(a) Procedures for setting terms and conditions of work, profit-sharing, training targets, equal opportunities policy and so on

(b) Disciplinary and grievance procedures, both individual and collective, including external arbitration and conciliation. (Individual disciplinary and grievance procedures were discussed in the Human Resource Management Course Book.)

(c) Recognition of trade unions (if applicable) to represent worker interests through the processes of collective bargaining and consultation

(d) Development of added or alternative mechanisms for employee representation and consultation (such as works councils, joint consultation committees and employee forums)

(e) Determination of the structure and scope of consultation and employee involvement in decision-making, within the framework of collective bargaining, partnership agreements, works councils, general HRM policies and so on.

1.2 Workers and their organisations

Trade unions

Definitions

A **trade union** is an organised association of employees who 'consist wholly or mainly of workers of one or more description and whose principal purposes include the regulation of relations between workers and employers' *(Trade Unions and Labour Relations (Consolidation) Act).*

An **independent trade union** is one which has been certified as being autonomous and financially self-supporting: not dominated by an employer because of the provision or withdrawal of financial or other support.

A single trade union might include members from different organisations in the same industry, and a single organisation might employ workers who belong to a number of different trade unions. Employees may be members of various unions, but the employer is not compelled to deal with a union unless it is 'recognised' for the purposes of collective bargaining or negotiation. The *Employment Relations Act* 1999 (Paragraph 2.6 below) introduced statutory provision for obtaining or enforcing recognition.

A firm may recognise a number of different unions in the workplace, to represent different categories of employees. Multi-unionism has significant drawbacks, however: encouraging demarcation disputes and the proliferation of work rules; competitive and therefore escalating pay settlements; and the cost and complexity of multiple bargaining time and machinery.

Firms desiring to simplify bargaining arrangements and secure greater flexibility and integration will often seek to negotiate a **sole recognition** or **single union agreement**, whereby only one union is recognised for the purpose of collective bargaining: workers who want representation must join this union. Sole recognition – and even more, the de-recognition of one union in favour of another – is, however, fraught with inter-union competition, and may not be perceived as genuinely representative of the interests of all staff. It is frequently achieved by a 'beauty contest approach', which arguably creates a situation in which unions must offer to fulfil the expectations of management in order to be granted recognition (and access to a fresh pool of members) rather than fulfilling the expectations of their members.

The primary functions carried out by a trade union are directly related to its objectives of improving the collective pay, conditions and job security of its members. Trade unions pursue their objectives through the processes of:

(a) **Collective bargaining** and negotiation (discussed in Chapter 5), which determines minimum standards to be applied to members covered by the resulting agreement

(b) **Joint consultation**: discussing, with representatives of management, issues of mutual concern (such as re-organisations, redundancies, health and safety)

(c) **Member services**: representation in grievance and disciplinary matters; obtaining sickness and accident benefits; advising on, and arranging access to, basic skills and workplace training (through Union Learning Representatives, as discussed in Chapter 3); legal advice and assistance.

Activity 1 **(15 minutes)**

What other activities of unions are you aware of, which are not directly connected to the achievement of its goals, but which might indirectly be effective in protecting members' rights?

The Trades Union Congress (TUC)

The TUC is a voluntary association of unions originally established in 1868. It holds an annual week-long congress or conference, for the purpose of debate, policy formation and the election of its general council. The TUC's purpose is:

(a) To formulate and express policy for the UK trade union movement as a whole

(b) To consult with industry and government bodies on issues affecting the trade union movement, and to lobby for relevant legislation

(c) To manage disputes between affiliated unions (eg over membership 'poaching' or job demarcation) through a Disputes Committee

(d) To intervene and try to effect a settlement in an industrial dispute, if invited to do so by the union involved

(e) To investigate complaints that an affiliated union's conduct is against the interest or policy of the congress.

The TUC has limited influence over its affiliates, however, through the threat of suspension or expulsion from the Congress. The autonomy of affiliates is still a key value.

We will discuss trade unions in more detail in Section 2. However, trade unions are not the only employee representatives with whom management may deal, formally or informally. There has been a trend towards non-unionised forums for consultation and participation. Again, these will be discussed in detail later (in Chapter 6), but we will survey some of the possibilities briefly here.

Other employee representative groups

Staff associations represent the employees (or groups of employees) within a particular organisation. They have been particularly popular among white-collar workers (eg in banking and insurance), for whom trade unionism was less socially acceptable.

The main reasons for employees to form a staff association are the desire for collective representation and/or negotiating powers (eg to respond to a specific threat, such as redundancies) – *without* the formality and ideological baggage of a trade union.

The majority of staff associations are recognised by employers for the purposes of consultation and negotiation. However, their narrow membership base and lack of funding limits their bargaining power.

Management generally prefer to deal with staff associations because they are less subject to third-party external interests: mutuality of interests may therefore be expected to be easier to achieve, with less external exposure, and staff associations may offer sufficient representation to head off demands for unionisation.

Most staff associations, however, are independent of the employer and provide a genuine alternative to trade unions in terms of employee representation.

Professional bodies and associations (eg the British Medical Association) may also represent the interests of their members in negotiation with employers, alongside their role as guardians of professional ethics and standards, educators and certifiers of practitioners and so on.

1.3 Employers and their organisations

Employers' associations and federations

Employers' associations are voluntary private groups of employers founded to facilitate trade, communication and representation in areas of common interest. Some are national bodies covering a whole industry (for example, the Engineering Employers Federation), while others are regional or specialised in their scope.

The largest UK employers' associations include the Engineering Employers' Federation (EEF), the Chemical Industries Association (CIA), the Road Haulage Association (RHA), the Federation of Master Builders (FMB), the Newspaper Society and the British Clothing Industry Association.

Employers' associations consist of companies of different sizes and organise themselves in different ways: most are consultative, rather than decision-making, bodies. Some give priority to trade matters, others to employee relations.

They were initially developed on an ad hoc basis in response to specific industrial disputes with the early trade unions, but by the end of the nineteenth century, in response to the growing influence of unionism, they adopted the federated approach to organisation at an industry/national level.

The role of the associations has declined with the increasing decentralisation of industrial relations processes: the growth in company- or plant-level bargaining, for example, and the decline of industry-wide agreements. Nevertheless, employers' associations still negotiate agreements at national level, especially in industries (such as electrical contracting and printing) which are dominated by small companies in competitive labour markets: national agreements provide industry frameworks and reduce price competition for skills. Moreover, employers wishing to influence EU policy must be part of an employers' association, which in turn may be affiliated to one of the EU-wide employer voices recognised by the EU Commission for the purposes of consultation and negotiation.

The main purposes of employers associations are:

(a) To give general help and advice on employee relations issues

(b) To represent members' views to political influencers and decision-making bodies (eg lobbying parliament)

(c) To assist member firms in the resolution of disputes (including representation at Employment Tribunals)

(d) To negotiate sectoral collective agreements (where applicable) with trade unions.

The Confederation of British Industry (CBI)

The Confederation of British Industry (CBI) was formed in 1965 as the main national federation of employers' associations in the UK, with the purpose of promoting British industry through political lobbying. Its main function is to influence policy on industry-related issues: it is not directly involved in employee relations processes, although it does maintain working relationships with the TUC, ACAS and other bodies.

1.4 Third parties

Third parties, such as government, arbitrators and judges (including the European Court of Justice) have an important bearing on industrial relations, because they set a framework for what employers and employees can and cannot do.

The UK government has established agencies such as the Advisory, Conciliation and Arbitration Service (ACAS) and Employment Tribunals, to assist or act as go-betweens in employment and industrial relations matters.

ACAS

According to the *Employment Protection Act 1975*, ACAS was designed to 'promote the improvement of industrial relations'. It is an independent body, governed by a Council whose members are appointed after consultation with worker and employer organisations.

ACAS has the ability to intervene at the request of employers and/or trade unions in the event of a possible or actual trade dispute. It may enquire into a complaint by a recognised trade union that insufficient information has been disclosed for collective bargaining purposes. It may also enquire on its own initiative into any industrial relations matter and publish its findings. It prepares and publishes Codes of Practice giving guidance for improving industrial relations (in areas such as disciplinary procedure).

ACAS may also be involved in individual conciliation cases, prior to hearing by tribunal. (It is frequently called in, for example, over equal opportunity and unfair dismissal complaints.)

Activity 2 **(10 minutes)**

Look up some definitions: what is the meaning of (a) conciliation (b) mediation and (c) arbitration? (Add the ways in which ACAS accomplishes these things, briefly, if you know.)

The Central Arbitration Committee

This body acts as arbitrator in disputes referred to it by ACAS. Under the Employment Relations Act 1999, it is called upon to make a ruling in cases where a union and an employer fail to reach agreement on union recognition or on the conduct of collective bargaining or on the establishment and operation of European Works Councils.

Employment Tribunals

Employment Tribunals (formed under the *Employment Tribunals Act 1996*) deal with most cases brought under employment law. They consist of an independent, legally-qualified chairperson, and two representative members, from the employer and the union. Their constitution is informal, but their decisions are legally binding. Evidence is given on oath, witnesses are called and legal representation is permitted as in a court of law. Appeals may be made (on points of law only) to the Employment Appeals Tribunal:

this is a formal court, consisting of a judge and lay members representing both sides of industry, and its decisions establish legal precedent.

Tribunals were discussed in the Human Resources Management Course Book.

INTERNATIONAL COMPARISON

In the **USA**, although the government plays a limited role in influencing collective agreements, third party intervention in negotiation and mediation (eg via the Federal Mediation and Conciliation Service) is widespread.

1.5 Other stakeholders

There is increasing public awareness of Corporate Social Responsibility (CSR) in relation to labour-related globalisation issues such as the use of child labour and sweatshops in developing nations, and the widening gap between 'fat cat' managerial pay and that of workers. These issues have been brought to the public's attention not by trade unions, but by pressure groups (non-government organisations, or NGOs) such as Oxfam, Anti-Slavery International and Clean Clothes.

Pressure groups have arguably become lead players in employment-related issues. Industries in sporting goods, and apparel, fashion and food retail are among the targets of widespread PR pressure, consumer protest and boycott in relation to labour practices.

'The challenges for unions and HR practitioners are different. Some unions are starting to form alliances with pressure groups. HR needs to take the initiative to defend its company's interests on employment-related issues as a whole and not to focus too closely on relations with the company's own employees. HR is also best placed to understand the new risks associated with the employment-related behaviour of contractors or companies that form part of the supply chain' (Wild, 2003).

Another major CSR issue, highlighted in recent years, is the environment, and issues such as climate change. Similar pressure is being placed on corporations – and HR professionals – to reduce greenhouse gas emissions, energy use and waste: this may affect HR policy in areas such as corporate travel, commuting and flexible working, office recycling and so on.

EXAMPLE

Appreciate the irony of this story…

'Oxfam is to continue sourcing anti-poverty wristbands from China, despite concerns about ethical standards. But the charity has stopped supplies from one manufacturer whose staff were found to be working under poor conditions.

'The move follows national media reports that some "Make Poverty History" bands had been manufactured at the Tat Shing Rubber Mfg Company, which forces new workers to pay "financial deposits". The coverage also reported how employees worked in unsuitable conditions and raised concerns over health and safety. Each of these points breach Oxfam's own Ethical Trading Initiative guidelines.

'The charity has stressed how the "mistake" highlights the importance for buyers to ensure goods are sourced at plants where conditions meet minimum standards.

'This should not mean a blanket rejection of sourcing in China. Instead we can work with the local company or factory to improve conditions. It is important that we engage to have a positive impact.'

(*Supply Management*, 23 June 2005)

FOR DISCUSSION

Whose 'business' is it how corporations treat their workers?

1.6 The role of the HR department

As in many other areas of HRM, it is often the line managers who have responsibility on a day-to-day basis for the implementation of industrial relations policy in regard to:

(a) Exchanging information with office representatives – say, to discuss changes in work procedures or newly-introduced rules

(b) Conducting disciplinary and grievance measures

(c) Implementing collective agreements on working procedures and conditions

(d) Managing interpersonal and team relations in such a way as to minimise potential conflict and preserve organisational authority in the face of collective labour strength.

However, there is a continuing role of HR specialists in developing policies which promote consistent decisions on industrial relations issues, especially since line managers may resist employee relations techniques in the belief that they will hamper their work and limit their flexibility.

We will discuss in Section 4 how HR policy affects industrial relations, and how the HRM approach ('employee relations') differs from the traditional approach ('industrial relations'). Here, we will look in more detail at the major player in traditional industrial relations: the trade unions.

2 TRADE UNIONS

2.1 Types of trade union

Unions are often distinguished as follows.

(a) **Craft and occupational unions**, which recruit employees who perform certain jobs. These include:

(i) White collar unions (employees in office work or desk jobs), and
(ii) Craft unions (manual workers skilled at a particular craft).

Examples include the British Airline Pilots Association (Balpa) and the National Union of Teachers.

(b) **Industrial unions**, which recruit all grades of employees employed in a particular industry. Examples include the National Union of Mineworkers and the Iron and Steel Trades Confederation.

(c) **General unions**, which organise workers from a variety of different jobs and industries. Examples include the Transport and General Workers Union (T&G) and GMB, the 'general' trade union.

Despite these different types, the UK system is essentially 'job-centred': the job an individual performs largely determines which union (s)he will join.

INTERNATIONAL COMPARISONS

- In **Germany**, trade unions are organised on industrial lines: one trade union represents all organised employees at a workplace, irrespective of their individual occupation. The German Trade Union Federation (DGB) is a non-political affiliation based on industrial unionism.
- In **Japan**, unions are mostly organised by company or establishment: an enterprise union consists of regular employees of a single firm, both white– and blue-collar. This has traditionally been supported by long-term career stability.
- In **France**, unions are mostly general unions, organised into five major confederations with broad divisions along politico-religious lines: socialist, communist, social democratic, Christian.
- Job- or occupation-centred unionism is a feature of **Anglo-Saxon countries** such as the UK, USA and Australasia.

2.2 Trade union representatives

Trade union representatives include:

(a) **Full-time paid officials**: 'organisers' or 'officers', employed by the union at district or regional level to carry out its policies under the direction of its national executive committee; and headquarters staff (financial, legal and administrative, under a 'general secretary')

(b) **Part-time voluntary officials**, elected to be branch officers of the union in a particular area

(c) **Workplace representatives** (shop stewards or staff representatives) who are employed by the organisation, but act on behalf of their fellow employees as their recognised representative. (Some very large firms with sensitive industrial relations may retain one or two employees on full pay to act in their union capacity full time.) **Shop stewards** are the link between the work group, the union officials and management: they require extensive knowledge of the union's service, employment and industrial relations law, ACAS and tribunal machinery, the policies and practices of the organisation, the role of managers and so on.

The structure of a union is **democratic**: local branch members elect representatives to a district or regional committee, which elect a national committee. The policy of the union is (theoretically) representative of the views of members, not of its leadership. However, the potential divergence between the goals and values of individual members and those of the organisation is just as great for a trade union as for a business. This view was given a political edge by the 1980s Conservative government's legislative support for the rights of individual union members (for example, secret balloting on use of union funds and industrial action). Its Industrial Relations Code of Practice stated that it should be the responsibility of the union to ensure that:

(a) Its members understand the organisation, policy and rules of the union

(b) Its members understand the powers and duties of the members themselves and those of their union representatives

(c) Its officials are adequately trained to look after their members' interest in an efficient and responsible way.

2.3 The rise, fall and rise of trade unionism

Early development

The UK trade union movement is the oldest in the world. Trade unions developed in the mid-nineteenth century, mainly as organisations of skilled workers in craft-dominated industries seeking to secure employment. In the latter half of the century, labourers and other unskilled workers also organised.

The first attempt to unite skilled and unskilled workers was Robert Owen's Grand National Consolidated Trades Union (1834). This collapsed following the transportation to Australia of the so-called 'Tolpuddle Martyrs': six members of the Friendly Society of Agricultural Labourers of Tolpuddle, Dorset, founded in 1833 to secure fair wages for its members, who were charged with administering unlawful oaths, and became the founding heroes of the trades union movement.

In 1851, the first successful national trade union, the Amalgamated Society of Engineers, was formed, and the Trades Union Congress (TUC) met for the first time in 1868.

Trade unions were finally granted legal status in 1871.

Rise...

Following legal status, more trades unions began to be formed, particularly by unskilled workers. The London dockers successfully struck in 1889 (for a wage of sixpence, ie 2 ½ pence, per hour!), encouraging others.

During the 1890s, the trades union movement supported the formation of the Labour Party, supplying funding (as it continues to do today). The Labour Representation Committee was formed in 1900 and renamed the Labour Party in 1906.

1926 saw a national strike by workers in Britain's major industries, lasting from 3-12 May: The General Strike. The TUC called out its members in support of the miners, who had refused to accept a reduction in wages. The strike involved over two million workers in transport, iron and steel, building, printing, gas and electricity. However, the government was able to keep essential services going, and the strike was forced to fold.

In 1945, however, Labour won a huge majority in the first post-war general election, and was able to introduce a programme of radical policies under Clement Attlee. The unions became increasingly powerful during the Labour term(s) in government. Trade union membership in the UK reached a peak of 13.29 million in 1979, also the year in which the number, duration and severity of strike actions reached their peak.

And fall…

During the 1980s and early '90s, the power of trade unions in the UK was affected by a number of factors.

(a) Declining membership and the increase in non-unionised organisations. This was partly due to the decline in manufacturing and the growth in the service sector where membership has traditionally been low. Meanwhile, competitive pressures resulted in employers' de-recognising of trade unions in order to end restrictive work rules and collective bargaining. Falling membership creates a vicious circle: weakening union effectiveness, which further depresses membership, and so on.

(b) Union concerns such as collective negotiation, occupational demarcations and work rules were being marginalised by HRM trends such as: negotiation of individual contracts; individual performance management and performance- or merit-related pay awards; multi-skilling and flexible working; direct communication policies; worker empowerment, involvement and participation schemes; the introduction of Japanese management and production techniques (collectivist, participative, low-conflict) and so on. The whole trend towards 'commitment'-based HRM, with a unitary perspective, suggested that the adversarial industrial relations model, associated with unionism, could be by-passed.

(c) The unions' power was intentionally weakened by Conservative governments from 1979 – 1997, through legislation such as:

  (i) The abolition of the 'closed shop', under which membership of a union could be made a condition of employment

  (ii) The requirement for secret balloting of union members when proposing industrial action, which gave support to the more moderate elements of the trade union movement

  (iii) The protection of individual union members' rights (including the right to refuse to participate in or support a strike)

  (iv) The right of employers to dismiss employees taking unofficial strike or other industrial action.

And rise…?

There has been a significant turnaround in the last few years in the number of union recognition agreements in force in the UK and the number and proportion of workers covered by such agreements.

This has been accelerated by:

(a) New recognition laws (see section 2.6)

(b) The Labour government's support for an industrial relations climate in which employers are less inclined to behave unilaterally, thus legitimising the union role in organisations

(c) Employer recognition that there is a positive business case for dealing with the workforce through unions, as a more efficient, positive and democratic method. Trade unions may be argued to fulfil a number of key managerial functions (Sisson & Storey, 2000):

  (i) An **agency** function, acting on behalf of large numbers of employees in their dealing with management, with benefits for consistency and management time/cost savings

  (ii) A **feedback** function, voicing the complaints and grievances of employees – which management need to be aware of

  (iii) A **stabilising** function, helping to manage workforce discontent by legitimising procedures and managerial prerogatives.

(d) Concerted recruitment drives, often supported by employers who have signed voluntary and partnership agreements with a union. 'At a workplace level, partnership means employers and trade unions working together to achieve common goals such as fairness and competitiveness. This more co-operative attitude on the part of trade unions, it is argued, has made employers more willing to recognise them and have a relationship with them' (Gennard & Judge, 2003).

The picture for unions is not all rosy, however. In 2008, trade union membership for employees in the UK fell to 27.4% – a continual decline in most industry sectors since 1998 (*Trade Union Membership 2008*, BERR).

2.4 The sources of trade union power

The power of a given trade union in bargaining and negotiating with employers will depend on a complex of factors.

(a) The **degree of support** for union actions from its members, and its ability to attract and maintain membership. This in turn may depend on a number of factors:

  (i) The conditions pertaining in the industry or organisation, the aspirations of members and hence the perceived advantages of trade union membership.

  (ii) Employment issues such as recessionary downsizing, or the introduction of new technology, which enhance the perceived importance of worker representation.

  (iii) Competition for members between unions, or between a union and a staff association.

(b) The **perceived success or failure** of the union in obtaining beneficial agreements for its members.

(c) The **bargaining environment**, including:

  (i) The **employer's HRM policies**. If terms and conditions are felt to be fair, good in comparison to market rates and so on, there will be little impetus for bargaining.

(ii) The **local labour market**. If there is a local shortage of the skill groups represented by the union, it will have greater bargaining power, but the reverse is also true: in time of high unemployment, the union movement is weakened. 'There is less talk about the quality of working life when there is little work to be had' (Huczynski & Buchanan, 2001).

(d) The culture of the union, and in particular its willingness to use industrial muscle. This resides primarily in the threat of withdrawal of labour in disputes (discussed in Chapter 5).

Activity 3 **(5 minutes)**

Why do you think the **size of the union** (number of members) has been left out of our account?

2.5 The law on trade union membership and activities

The **closed shop** (whereby an employee had to be a member of a relevant union in order to obtain or retain a job) was stripped of all legal protection under the Employment Acts 1988: dismissal for non-membership of a union was automatically to be deemed unfair, and industrial action to create or maintain closed shop practices lost its legal immunity.

On the other hand, further legislation has protected the freedom of individuals to join the union of their choice. No action may be taken to compel people to be members of a union, nor to deter them. Nor can employees be prevented from participation in union activities at an appropriate time: if the union is both independent and recognised by the employer, there is a further right to reasonable time off for union activities.

Individual union members' rights (*Employment Act 1988, Employment Relations Acts 1999 and 2004*) include the following.

(a) Individuals have the right not to be unjustifiably disciplined by a union (eg by fines, expulsion, withdrawal of benefits or blacklisting) for refusing to strike, for crossing a picket line or for initiating or inciting legal actions against the union.

(b) Individuals cannot be dismissed for taking official, lawfully-organised industrial action in the first 12 weeks.

(c) Employees covered by a collective workplace agreement cannot be forced to sign an individual contract.

(d) Blacklisting of, or discrimination against, trade union members is outlawed.

(e) Improper campaigning activity by unions and employers, in relation to recognition/de-recognition ballots, is defined (to prevent intimidation).

Activity 4 **(15 minutes)**

Why do you think the closed shop existed, and why was it abolished?

The law on strikes is discussed in Chapter 5. The* Employment Relations Act 1999 *also introduced major new provisions for statutory trade union recognition, the first time this has been subject to UK law. We will look at the implications for industrial relations.

2.6 Trade union recognition

Under the *Employment Relations Act 1999*, independent trade unions can apply in writing to an employer to be granted recognition. Recognition may be:

(a) **Voluntary**, if a ballot (triggered by 10% union membership within the proposed bargaining unit) returned a 40% 'yes' vote, or

(b) **Automatic**, if more than 50% (plus one person) of the bargaining unit are 'full and conscious' members of the union.

If the union and the employer fail to reach agreement on recognition or on the conduct of collective bargaining, the Central Arbitration Committee (CAC) can make a ruling.

Reports from the CAC suggest that trade unions are using applications for statutory recognition as bargaining tools to win voluntary agreements from employers. Several hundred new recognition deals per year have been signed since 1999. High-profile 'scalps' include Virgin Atlantic, which after many years of refusal entered discussions on recognition with the pilots' union Balpa. The overwhelming majority of trade union agreements have been voluntary agreements for recognition, covering at least pay, hours and holidays.

There are also a small but significant number of **non-traditional deals** stipulating that bargaining should be conducted through company councils or staff forums, on which there may also be representation for union members. This usually happens where union recognition is added to existing consultation procedures: examples include Monarch Airlines' agreement with the AEEU and Eurotunnel's with the T&G.

> The proposition unions are putting to employers is different from what it was a generation ago. More are approaching companies with an offer that seeks to provide workforce representation in a way that's not necessarily going to make life disruptive for the employer. They are asking: 'How can we work with you?' We've been surprised at the extent to which the voluntary approach seems to be the dominant one. *(People Management,* September 2000)

The **Employment Rights Act 2004** made some amendments to the 1999 Act, including the following.

(a) Improving the operation of the statutory recognition procedures. This includes clarifying 'appropriate bargaining units' and 'topics' appropriate for collective bargaining and allowing unions to communicate with workers earlier in the process.

(b) Tackling intimidation of workers during recognition and de-recognition ballots.

(c) Extending the protection of employees taking official and lawfully organised industrial action: extending the 'protected period' (during which dismissal is automatically unfair) to 12 weeks, and exempting 'lock out' days from this period (so employers can't justify dismissals by preventing employees from returning to work for 12 weeks!).

Weblinks

You may like to explore some trade-union related sites.

The TUC
►► **http://www.tuc.org.uk**

Unions 21, the trade union 'think tank'
►► **http://www.unions21.org.uk**

Aslef (the main train drivers union)
►► **http://www.aslef-org.uk**

The Communication Workers Union
►► **http://cwu.org**

The GMB ('Britain's General Union')
►► **http://www.gmb.org.uk**

The Commonwealth Trade Union Council
►► **http://www.commonwealthtuc.ord**

International Centre for Trade Union Rights
►► **http://ictur.labournet.org**

Industrial relations can be contentious, with both legitimate differences and ingrained prejudices on either side. We will now look briefly at the ideological framework underlying industrial relations.

3 THE IDEOLOGICAL FRAMEWORK

3.1 Unitary and pluralist frames of reference

Fox (1975) identified three broad ideologies which are involved in industrial relations.

(a) **Unitary ideology**. All members of the organisation, despite their different roles, have common objectives and values which unite their efforts. Workers are loyal, and the prerogative of management is accepted as paternal, and in everyone's best interests. Unions are a useful channel of communication, but are no longer strictly necessary: they can indeed be counterproductive in offering support to potentially disruptive elements.

> Any business must mould a true team and weld individual efforts into a common effort. Each member of the enterprise contributes something different, but they must all contribute towards a common goal. Their efforts must all pull in the same direction, without friction, without unnecessary duplication of effort.
>
> (Drucker, 1955)

(b) **Pluralist ideology.** Organisations are political coalitions of individuals and groups which have their own interests. Management has to create a workable structure for collaboration, taking into account the objectives of all the various interest groups or stakeholders in the organisation. A mutual survival strategy, involving the control of conflict through compromise, can be made acceptable in varying degrees to all concerned.

(c) **Radical ideology**. This primarily Marxist ideology argues that there is an inequality of power between the controllers of economic resources (shareholders and managers) and those who depend on access to those resources (wage earners). Those in power exploit the others by indoctrinating them to accept the legitimacy of their rights to power, and thus perpetuate the system. Conflict between these strata of society – the proletariat and the bourgeoisie – does not aim for mutual survival, but for revolutionary change: bringing down the system.

> The history of all societies hitherto is the history of class struggles. Freeman and slave, patrician and plebeian, lord and serf, guildmaster and journeyman, in a word, oppressor and oppressed, stood in constant opposition to one another, carried on an uninterrupted, now hidden, now open fight.
>
> (Marx and Engels, *The Communist Manifesto*, 1888)

FOR DISCUSSION

Which of the above views do you subscribe to?

3.2 Different stakeholder interests

'Them and us' attitudes have traditionally been ingrained in UK industry, partly because of class-consciousness. You should be aware that they are to an extent inevitable, given the tendency of people to draw boundaries round any group they are in. It should also be remembered that there are different interest groups *within* both management and employees as well as *between* them. For example, there may be a clash of interests between HR managers aiming for the stability, quality and flexibility of the workforce, in accordance with ethical HR practice, and operations managers aiming for immediate efficiency gains through 'lean production'. The interests of white-collar, craft and unskilled workers may clash over differentials, status and demarcation boundaries.

However, the root of union-management conflict, as we have seen, frequently lies in genuine inequities and artificial status distinctions. We have already discussed ways in which less divisive systems (such as single status agreements, salaried status for all grades and Japanese management practices) are available to emphasise a unitary rather than a pluralistic perspective.

According to Gennard and Judge (2003), 'the rationale for employee relations is to solve the problem that in a labour market the buyers (employers) and sellers (employees) have an endemic conflict of interests over the "prices" at which they wish to exchange their services.' In this view, there is a perpetual **trade off** between what the employer wants (productivity, quality, functional flexibility, numerical flexibility and/or labour stability according to circumstance and so on) and what the employee wants in return (a certain level of pay and incentives, family-friendly policies, opportunities for development, job security and/or mobility according to circumstances and so on).

Employee relations therefore recognises differences (if not conflicts) of interest. Gennard and Judge quote a Recognition Procedural Agreement involving the Scottish Carpet Workers Union which includes the following general principles.

> The Union recognises management's responsibility to plan, organise and manage the company's operation.
>
> The company recognises the Union's responsibility to represent the interests of their [sic] members and to maintain or improve their terms and conditions of employment and work within the constraints imposed on the plant by corporate policy and finance.

3.3 Shared stakeholder interests

Trade unions have a vested interest in the success of the organisation to which their members belong because unless the organisation prospers, the job security, pay and benefits of their members will be compromised. Likewise, employers have a vested interest in the continuing commitment and welfare of employees, in order to maintain the viability of the business through the availability, quality and competitiveness of goods and services.

Sir Ken Jackson (*People Management*, September 2000) writes:

> It is clear that unions need to improve their ability to support their members. Our aim is to secure a better deal for them by adding value to their employers. We want to contribute to the success of the company by applying our representational talents with honesty, passion and industrial knowledge... It is only when managers are given intelligent, coherent criticism that they think through all the implications of their decisions. Equally, on many occasions, an informed union organisation will support managers' decisions and give them added credibility with the workforce.

3.4 Co-operation

According to the radical perspective, co-operation is merely collaboration in perpetuating oppression. According to the pluralist perspective, however, it is a negotiated process of mutual survival, taking into account the needs of the various stakeholders in the organisation. And according to the unitary perspective, it is the natural mode of business relations and achieves greater productivity and satisfaction for all parties than conflict or competition. Whatever your opinion, it is worth bearing in mind the following points.

(a) **Co-operation has a rational appeal**. It is demonstrable that a suitable number of people co-operating on a task will achieve a better result than one person doing the same task (synergy may enable 2+2 to equal 5) and that groups of co-operating individuals have higher productivity than groups of competing individuals. *However,* it has also been demonstrated that this is not always the case: collaboration can adversely affect individual and group performance, because of group norms, the distraction of group maintenance processes and the tendency of cohesive groups to become blinkered, self-protecting and risky in their decision-making.

(b) **Co-operation has an emotional appeal**. It incorporates values about unity, teamwork, comradeship and belonging: as such, it is a useful cornerstone to the communication of corporate culture. *However*, Charles Handy (among others) has suggested that organisations are too quick to label and discourage differences, argument and competition as 'conflict': these are not only natural and inevitable (pluralist perspective) but potentially beneficial and fruitful (Handy, 1993).

(c) **Co-operation is a common cultural value-cluster**: collectivist cultures such as Japan and Sweden emphasise inter-dependence. *However,* individualist cultures such as the UK and USA value independence more highly.

> **Activity 5** **(15 minutes)**
>
> How might conflict in the form of differences, argument and competition be beneficial and fruitful for an organisation?

4 EMPLOYEE RELATIONS

4.1 HRM and industrial relations

Guest (2001) described four possible orientations to industrial relations strategy as follows.

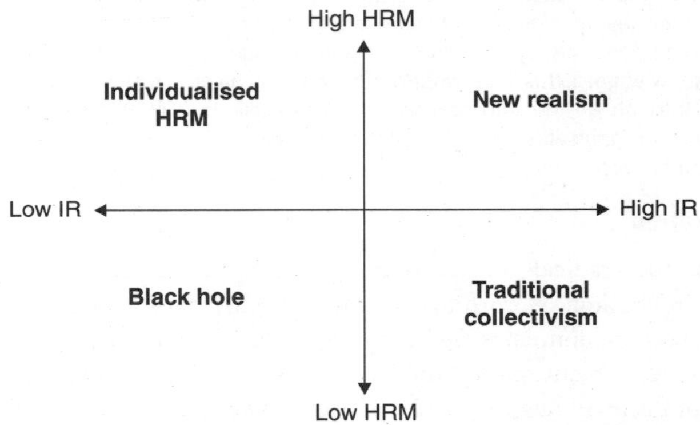

Figure 4.1: Guest's orientations for industries relations strategy

(a) **The new realism:** *high emphasis on HRM and industrial relations.* Companies such as Nissan and Toshiba have initiated collaborative arrangements, extended consultation processes and moves towards single status, in order to facilitate greater flexibility, more multi-skilling, the removal of demarcations and improvements in quality.

(b) **Traditional collectivism:** *emphasis on industrial relations without HRM.* Unions provide useful, well-established channels for communication and the handling of grievance/discipline/safety issues: it is easier to continue to operate a traditional pluralist industrial relations arrangement.

(c) **Individualised HRM:** *emphasis on HRM without industrial relations.* This is an 'essentially piecemeal and opportunistic' approach which is only common among North-American firms.

(d) **The black hole:** *no industrial relations.* HRM is not considered a policy priority for management, but neither is there seen to be a need for a traditional industrial relations system.

It has been argued that a thorough-going 'HRM' approach – with its unitary perspective and commitment-based strategies – renders the traditional 'industrial relations' approach irrelevant and marginalises the traditional roles of the trade union.

Activity 6 **(15 minutes)**

(a) What are the features of employee relations in the 'industrial relations' model and the 'HRM' model?

(b) What kinds of HRM policies, would reduce the perceived need for trade union representation?

The TUC's HRM Taskforce reported in 1994, however, that it found no direct relationship between HRM techniques and anti-unionism. In fact, HRM was most prevalent in unionised workplaces. Taskforce chair Bernadette Hillan said: 'If an employer is really trying to improve business performance, is committed to involving workers in the running of the organisation and is seeking to develop a real partnership with recognised trade unions, then HRM and collective bargaining can work in harmony.' She did, however, admit that some employers were using at least the language of HRM as an excuse to de-recognise unions.

The 2000 TUC conference was likewise told by its general secretary, John Monks, that: 'The most successful companies in the UK have the very best management practice, where unions are strong and working in partnership with management.'

FOR DISCUSSION

'One of the unsubstantiated myths in employee relations has been the idea that non-unionism is the panacea for business success, for which organisations such as Marks & Spencer and IBM are put forward as prime examples.

There will always be a debate between those who see trade unions as a negative influence and those, like most of our European partners, who see rights at work (including trade union membership and collective bargaining) as part of an important social dimension to working relationships.

Although the debate about unionism versus non-unionism continues, the real question tends to be ignored. That is – is it easier to manage with unions or without unions? … How many of the companies who yearn for non-union status would be prepared to make the investment in people management that the organisations that they envy have done?'

(Gennard & Judge, 2003)

Debate the issues raised here, justifying your views.

4.2 From 'industrial relations' to 'employee relations'

The Industrial Relations Services have identified four approaches to industrial relations (as cited by Armstrong, 2009).

(a) **Adversarial**: the organisation decides what it wants to do and employees are expected to fit in. Employees only exercise power by refusing to co-operate.

(b) **Traditional**: a good day-to-day working relationship, but management proposes and the workforce reacts through its elected representatives.

(c) **Partnership**: the organisation involves employees in the drawing up and execution of organisation policies, but retains the right to manage.

(d) **Power sharing**: employees are involved in both day-to-day and strategic decision-making.

Definition

> **Employee relations** 'consist of all those areas of HRM that involve general relationships with employees, through collective agreements where trade unions are recognised [industrial relations] and/or through commonly applied policies for employee involvement and communications' (Armstrong, 2000).

According to Armstrong, employee relations strategy will be concerned with how to:

(a) Build **stable and co-operative relationships** with employees that minimise conflict

(b) Achieve **commitment** through employee involvement and communications processes

(c) Develop **mutuality** – a common interest in achieving the organisation's goals through the development of organisational cultures based on shared values between management and employees.

He suggests that such strategies will result in the following kinds of policies.

(a) Changing forms of recognition, including single union recognition or de-recognition

(b) New bargaining structures, including decentralisation or single-table bargaining (discussed in Chapter 5)

(c) The achievement of increased levels of commitment through involvement or participation – giving employees a voice

(d) Deliberately by-passing trade union representatives to communicate directly with employees

(e) Increasing the extent to which management controls operations in such areas as flexibility

(f) Generally improving the employee relations climate in order to produce more harmonious and co-operative relationships

(g) Developing a 'partnership' with trade unions (discussed in Chapter 6), recognising that employees are stakeholders and that it is to the advantage of both parties to work together.

EXAMPLE 1

Strike Free: New Industrial Relations in Britain by Philip Bassett (1986) illustrated the height of the 'anti-union' phase of HRM in the UK. The following was the experience of the (then) leading-edge computer company, IBM.

Company management attribute the good employee relations to IBM's belief in respect for the individual. One aspect of this philosophy is that IBM does not recognise trade unions for collective bargaining purposes. To do so, they believe, would imply that without trade unions employees' interests would be neglected. Management are convinced that the company's record disproves such a belief.

IBM does not discourage its employees from becoming members of trade unions, but very few of them do so. Even of those who do, a significant minority are against collective bargaining. Pay in IBM is not a collective matter for employees; instead, the company conducts its own confidential survey of comparable companies and determines salary ranges centrally. There is scope for line managers to recommend increases for specific individuals based on merit.

The other traditional function of trade unions at plant level is to assist their members over the hurdles of the employer's grievance system. IBM believe that their own internal complaints procedures, which allow an individual to take a grievance to the very highest levels of management, remove the need for any union involvement.

Other companies, looking at IBM's industrially harmonious, strike-free, non-union record, have asked how they could emulate it. The answer given by a former personnel director of the company is simple: 'You start 30 years ago.'

EXAMPLE 2

Canadian-owned Sheerness Steel, Kent, is the first company in its industry to have de-recognised unions, led by the Iron and Steel Trades Confederation (ISTC), as part of a change to a single status company. According to the personnel director: 'We have become a single status company with personal contracts, salaries, performance-related pay and no defined jobs – people do whatever they are trained to do. We realised that we no longer had anything to debate or discuss with the unions and that they were no longer necessary.'

However, according to the ISTC, the workforce is not happy. Local conditions of high unemployment 'had made it difficult for members to withstand company pressure to take personal contracts'. The change to salaried work means that employees have lost overtime payments which, according to the ISTC, has severely affected their earnings. On the other hand, many of the old disciplinary problems, such as being late, are no longer a problem: just as well, perhaps, since the unions are no longer even allowed to represent individual members in disciplinary cases...'

(*Personnel Management Plus*, September 1992)

FOR DISCUSSION

Do the examples cited above reflect a genuine HRM approach to employee relations?

Chapter roundup

- Industrial relations comprises all the rules, practices and conventions governing interactions between managements and their workforces, normally involving collective employee representation and bargaining.
- Employee relations consist of all these areas of HRM that involve general relationships with employees, including industrial relations and employee involvement and communication.
- The stakeholders in industrial relations include: management and/or employers' associations, worker representatives (trade unions, staff associations or other forms of representation) and third parties, such as ACAS, Employment Tribunals and a range of non-government organisations.
- Trade unions may be craft/occupational, general or industrial. After a period of declining membership (accelerated by HRM policies, the decline of manufacturing and Conservative government policy) the political climate and statutory recognition laws have shown an upswing in unionism.
- There are three basic perspectives on industrial relations: unitary, pluralist and radical.

Quick quiz

1 What is an independent trade union?

2 What are the purposes of employers' associations?

3 How might wider society be involved in employee relations in a firm?

4 Distinguish between craft, industrial and general unions.

5 What is a shop steward?

6 Give four reasons for the recent turnaround in the number of workers covered by union recognition agreements.

7 What was the closed shop and what happened to it?

8 Distinguish between the unitary and pluralist frames of reference.

9 In what ways might management and workers be said to have:

(a) Different interests, and
(b) Common interests

10 Outline Guest's four orientations to industrial relations strategy.

Answers to quick quiz

1 One which has been certified as being autonomous and financially self-supporting, not dominated by an employer. (see paragraph 1.2)

2 To give help and advice on employee relations issues; to represent members' views to political influencers; to assist in dispute resolution; to negotiate sectoral agreements. (para 1.3)

3 Through pressure groups seeking to oppose exploitative labour relations. In a wider sense, in demanding corporate social responsibility. (para 1.5)

4 Craft unions recruit employees who perform certain jobs. Industrial unions recruit all grades of employees in a particular industry. General unions organise workers from a variety of different jobs and industries. (para 2.1)

5 A workplace union representative: the link between the work group, union officials and management. (para 2.2)

6 Statutory recognition; Labour government support for partnership; recognition of unions as a useful and efficient mechanism for employee relations; increasing recruitment, supported by single union and partnership agreements. (para 2.3)

7 An employee had to be a member of a particular union to secure or retain employment. The closed shop was stripped of legal support: dismissal for non-membership was made automatically unfair, selection on membership discriminatory and industrial action in support of a closed shop unlawful. (para 2.5)

8 Unitary: all members of the organisation, despite their different roles, have common interests and objectives which unites their efforts. The management prerogative is recognised as being in everyone's best interests.

Pluralist: organisations are political coalitions of individuals and groups which inevitably have their own interests. Management has to take into account the objectives of all the various stakeholders in the organisation, to develop a strategy of mutual compromise and survival. (para 3.1)

9 Basically, differences arise from the labour market: trading off the objectives of buyers (management) and sellers (workers) of labour. Common interests arise from both sides' vested interest in the survival and prosperity of the organisation. (see paragraphs 3.2 and 3.3)

10 New realism: high emphasis on HRM and industrial relations eg through partnership agreements.

Traditional collectivism: emphasis on industrial relations without HRM eg through collective bargaining.

Individualised HRM: HRM without industrial relations eg through individual contracts.

Black hole: no HRM or industrial relations eg authoritarian management. (para 4.1)

Answers to activities

1 (a) Lobbying politicians to obtain legislation to improve conditions of work (eg the minimum wage)

(b) Developing political affiliations with other trade unions, to create a power base for achieving political influence

(c) Providing financial support for a sympathetic political party (traditionally, the Labour Party)

(d) Establishing non-negotiatory processes for sharing management decision-making: eg by joint consultative committees or partnership agreements

(e) Providing welfare help and support for members: funding during industrial action, say

2 (a) Conciliation (getting conflicting parties together for informal discussion to resolve a dispute)

(b) Mediation (providing a mediator or mediation board, which hears arguments and makes proposals and recommendations as a basis for settlement)

(c) Arbitration (assisting in the appointment of independent arbitrators who make a binding ruling)

3 Size is a variable insignificant in itself: the Union's credibility rests on size as a proportion of potential membership. The threat of industrial action even by a large union would be hollow if its membership represented a very small proportion of workers in the relevant organisation or sector. A union which is small in terms of membership numbers may still have a very strong negotiating position if its members are of an occupational category which is significant to the organisation or national life (eg nurses, firemen).

4 The closed shop was encouraged by unions as a means of increasing their membership and bargaining power within a company. It was supported by some managements as a way of facilitating single-union agreements. Closed shops were criticised for interfering with individual rights of choice; constraining management decision-making on recruitment and retention; and strengthening the bargaining power of unions to the detriment of industrial relations.

5 (a) Differences allow for diversity of talents, viewpoints, ideas: necessary for innovation, problem-solving, understanding human dynamics, flexibility. Differences reflect the diversity of the customer base: conformity may blinker the organisation to potential needs or problems. Suppression of diversity may cause stress and resentment.

(b) Argument is useful to clear the air, help divergent viewpoints to emerge, encourage empathy with different viewpoints: extremely helpful in conflict resolution, in change management (bringing resistance into the open), in encouraging emotional intelligence.

(c) Controlled competition between teams has been demonstrated to increase team cohesion/co-operation and motivation and improve performance. Competition tied to incentives is a powerful energiser of performance (particularly in individualistic cultures).

6 (a) IR = low trust, collectivist, pluralist. HRM = high trust, individualist, unitarist.

(b) Examples include: direct voluntary communication and consultation on matters which will affect employees; worker involvement techniques; fair, consistent and transparent discipline and grievance handling; equitable and non-discriminatory recruitment, selection, appraisal and reward systems; health, safety and welfare policies clearly aimed at problem-solving and worker protection; programmes at improving the work environment; flexible remuneration packages (such as cafeteria benefits) encouraging individual aspirations and priorities.

Chapter 5:

INDUSTRIAL RELATIONS PROCESSES

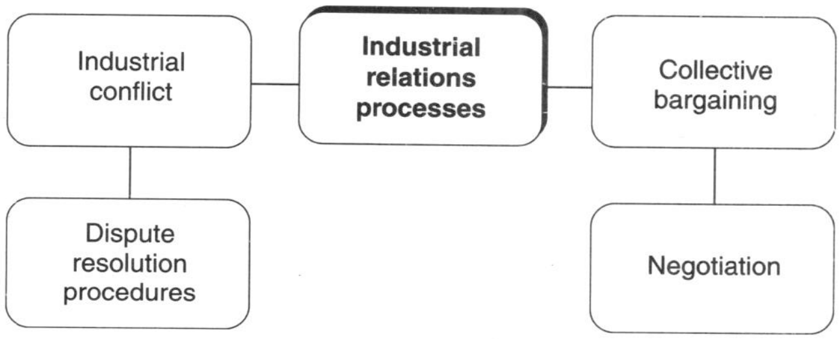

Introduction

In this chapter we explore some of the key processes in industrial relations: collective bargaining, and the related strategies and skills of negotiation and the management of industrial disputes.

In each of these areas, we will see signs of the shift towards a unitarist perspective discussed in Chapter 4, while at the same time recognising the differing interests of stakeholders in the organisation. Even industrial conflict must be managed in the context of an on-going relationship. This perspective is typified in the various measures taken to involve employees in decision-making, under the general banner of 'participation' and 'involvement': this area will be covered separately in Chapter 6.

Your objectives

In this chapter you will learn about the following.

(a) Different types of collective dispute

(b) Dispute procedures and the resolution of conflict

(c) The nature and scope of collective bargaining

(d) Negotiation processes and strategy

1 INDUSTRIAL CONFLICT

1.1 Types of collective dispute

Individual disputes against employers are covered by disciplinary and grievance procedures as discussed in the Human Resources Management Course Book.

We have already seen in Chapter 4 that there are deep-rooted ideologies of conflict embedded in industrial relations in the UK. **Collective disputes** typically involve pay, conditions of employment, job security or breach of contracts and negotiated agreements.

According to the *Employment Act 1982*, a 'lawful trade dispute' is one between workers and their own employers, wholly or mainly about work related matters, and *not:*

- Demarcation and other inter-union disputes
- Disputes between workers and employers other than their own
- Disputes other than those mainly connected with pay and conditions or
- Disputes overseas.

1.2 Industrial action

Industrial action in pursuance of a dispute may take a number of forms (discussed below), but are classified on four basic dimensions.

(a) **Official** action is supported by the trade union representatives of the employees in dispute, and conducted according to union procedure, including secret balloting of members.

(b) **Unofficial** action is taken by a part of the workforce without recognition and support from union officials and without balloting and approval procedures.

(c) **Primary** action is aimed at the employer with whom the participating union is in dispute.

(d) **Secondary** action is aimed at employers who trade with firms in dispute, but who are not directly involved in the dispute themselves.

Activity 1 **(15 minutes)**

What do you think might be the purpose of threatening or implementing industrial action?

EXAMPLE

In September 2003, members of the Communication Workers Union (CWU) voted against a national strike against Royal Mail following a pay deal which offered a productivity-linked 14.5% pay rise. (Even so, Royal Mail workers in London subsequently staged a series of 24 hour strikes over the London Weighting allowance.)

In May 2007, the postal group offered a pay freeze for the year (amidst planned cost cuts of £350 million), cutting weekend and night-shift working at many mail centres. The CWU referred to the moves as a 'cost cutting frenzy' and accused Royal Mail of blaming competition in the postal market for a 'slash and burn' approach to pay and working conditions.

Royal Mail countered that its workers were paid too highly compared with the industry average – although in 2006 it signed an agreement to improve pay. The CWU is fighting for pay to be brought into line with the national average – which would require a 27% increase.

In June 2007, the CWU called a one-day national strike accusing Royal Mail of not taking their grievances seriously. Post Office staff as well as Royal Mail staff would be called out, following a 77% vote of support from union members.

Royal Mail was 'astonished' and 'disappointed' by the threat.

(*People Management*, 26 April & 22 June 2007)

In August 2009, up to 25,000 postal workers were called out on a series of strikes across Britain – the biggest disruption to Royal Mail deliveries since the 2007 national stoppage. Workers protested against 'panic-driven' cuts to pay, jobs and services, said the CWU. Royal Mail condemned the action, which it said would damage customer confidence and 'undermine the entire UK postal industry' at a time when mail volumes are falling by nearly 10% year on year. The company also disputed the number of strikers, putting it at 12,000.

The CWU accused Royal Mail of imposing changes on staff. The company accused the union of reneging on the modernisation deal that ended the 2007 strike.

And so it goes ...

http://www.guardian.co.uk/uk/2009/Aug/06/postal-strike-royal-mail

---

Definition

Strike action is the withholding of labour in the course of a dispute with management.

Various forms of primary industrial action by union members (in order of severity) include the following.

(a) **Withdrawal of co-operation** by the union (eg refusal to participate in disciplinary procedures).

(b) **Insistence on formal rights** by the union (eg raising trivial infringements as grievance issues, insistence on taking time off or limiting overtime, where there would normally be informal flexibility).

(c) A **work-to-rule or go-slow**: employees follow official work procedures and rules to the letter, thereby reducing productivity without doing anything to justify disciplinary action by management. This also highlights the extent to which management take for granted the commitment and voluntary contribution of employees.

(d) A **ban on overtime** and weekend working to restrict productivity, often highlighting issues of work organisation.

(e) A **token withdrawal of labour**: for example, a one-day strike by the union membership in the workforce, as a protest against management's unwillingness to make further concessions in negotiation. These may be repeated over a period of time, in order to provide a recurring disruption to the organisation's operations without a complete loss of pay: 24-hour strikes by Royal Mail workers in 2003 is one example.

(f) **Indefinite strike action** by the entire union membership in the workforce, either at national level, company level or plant level: the 1984 miners' strike is a historic example.

(g) **Picketing**: striking workers maintain a presence outside the employer's premises (a 'picket line'). The aim of the picket line is to highlight the protest and to inform and solicit the support of workers attempting to enter the workplace. In practice, this often takes the form of active discouragement and intimidation of strike-breakers, replacement workers and others. The Employment Act 1982 protects unions and their members against most civil and criminal actions 'in contemplation or furtherance of a trade dispute', including picketing at or near the place of work with a purpose that is 'peacefully to obtain or communicate information, or peacefully to persuade a person to work or not to work'. Secondary picketing (of organisations not involved in the dispute) is not protected, however.

Activity 2 **(5 minutes)**

What are the corresponding 'industrial sanctions' which might be used by **management** in furtherance of an industrial dispute? Why might these be used as a 'last resort'?

The **threat** of applying industrial sanctions may be sufficient to make either or both of the parties adjust their position in a dispute, it being in the interests of neither party to incur the heavy costs of such sanctions – particularly if there is unlikely to be a successful outcome.

1.3 Statistics on strikes

Official statistics on the use of industrial sanctions in the UK only cover strikes. They measure:

(a) The frequency (number) of strikes

(b) The size of strikes (that is, the number of workers involved)

(c) The duration of strikes (that is, the number of working days lost) – since this figure on its own may give a distorted impression if there are a few very long strikes. For example, the 1984 miners' strike accounted for 83% of the total number of working days lost to strikes in that year!

All three measures peaked in 1979 (2,125 stoppages in progress, 4.6 million workers involved, and 29.4 million working days lost – of which 54% were accounted for by a strike of engineering workers). Most of these measures have continued to fall, with fluctuations according to the number of workers involved.

- In the year 2000, there were 212 stoppages, involving 182,000 workers and a loss of 499,000 lost working days.
- In 2008, there were 144 stoppages, involving 511,200 workers and a loss of 758,900 working days. 99% of working days lost were due to pay disputes.

(*Economic and Labour Market Review, 2008, vol 3, no 6)*

1.4 The law on strikes

Relevant provisions include the following.

(a) Official industrial action requires the **secret balloting** of all affected members. Seven days' notice must be given to an employer of a union's intention to ballot its members on industrial action.

(b) In the course of a lawful and duly balloted trade dispute, the trade union, its officials and participants in the dispute are immune from legal action. However, members of the public have the right to apply for a court order restraining a union from taking *unlawful* industrial action.

(c) **Picketing** carries legal immunity only if the pickets consist of employees who normally work at the premises, former employees (if the dispute concerns their termination), and employees who have no fixed place of work or who cannot picket their own place of work (and who therefore picket the premises from which their work is administered). Picketing solely to obtain or communicate information is not unlawful, but may become so if it involves obstruction of the public highway or breach of the peace. Secondary action of any kind is unlawful.

(d) An individual may not be unjustifiably disciplined by a union (eg by fines, expulsion, withdrawal of benefits or blacklisting) for **refusing** to strike or go slow if by so doing (s)he would be in breach of contract, or for crossing a picket line.

(e) It is unlawful to **dismiss strikers** for the first twelve weeks of a strike.

EXAMPLE

'The 250 **British Airways** staff who staged an unofficial walkout [in July 2003] certainly achieved the profile they would have wished for.

'The dispute provoked furore among customers left stranded at Heathrow airport, cost BA £40 million and also marked the beginning of days of deadlock in talks between management and staff.

'Many have been unsympathetic to the reason for the strike, which centred around the introduction of an electronic clocking-in system.

'While members of the public remained largely indifferent, some fellow colleagues described it as a "piffling issue".

'But analysts and experts have warned the significance of this strike should not be underestimated. What is critical, they have said, is that in this era of partnership working and general lack of rebellion, staff reached a point of such desperation they were willing to take the drastic action of staging a strike without their unions' backing. It demonstrates the severity of the breakdown in relations between management and staff. ...

'Mike Emmott, the CIPD's head of employee relations, agrees that this raises questions about people management practices at BA.

' "Workers do not take such drastic action as to walk out when they feel that they have trust in their management, when they feel listened to and when they feel that their best interests are at heart," he says.

' "Management has been saying that the scheme is simply about turning the paper-based system into an electronic one and that the workforce should trust them, but the simple fact is that the workforce doesn't believe them," he adds.'

(Watkins, 2003 (d))

1.5 No strike agreements

The 'right to strike' in enshrined in employment law. However, no-strike agreements may be made by voluntary agreement between employers and unions. *The Trade Union and Labour Relations Act 1974* states that a no-strike clause in a collective agreement can only be made part of individual contracts of employment when the agreement provides expressly and in writing for its inclusion, and when the agreement is made reasonably accessible to employees at the workplace.

No-strike clauses effectively deprive union negotiators of the threat of strike action in the event of breakdown in bargaining, and arguably deprive workers of one of their only sources of power in the employment relationship. They therefore tend to be attached to collective agreements which support the managerial prerogative, such as single-union and partnership agreements.

FOR DISCUSSION

Do you think certain categories of worker should be deprived of the right to strike, in the national interest? If so, which? (Think of times when your own life was disrupted by strike action.)

Having seen how industrial disputes arise, we will now consider how they may be resolved.

2 DISPUTE RESOLUTION PROCEDURES

2.1 Dispute procedures

Detailed procedural agreements on disputes are generally made during collective bargaining or other (non-union) negotiated agreements. A typical dispute procedure would provide for the 'escalating' involvement of more senior representatives of both sides, with a guarantee of new industrial action until all stages have been followed through.

(a) Meeting of union representative and middle management

(b) Meeting of district union officer and senior management

(c) Meeting of regional and then national officials of the union and employers' association (in national disputes)

(d) Conciliation (if required)

(e) Mediation (if required)

(f) Agreement to abide by the decision of an independent arbitrator (as a last resort, since the decision then passes out of the hands of the parties involved).

If dispute procedures fail to re-open negotiation or resolve conflict, the parties may consider calling in ACAS to offer the services of conciliation, mediation and arbitration.

2.2 The role of ACAS

Conciliation is a voluntary process of discussion, facilitated by ACAS conciliators whose role is to make constructive suggestions, provide information and manage the process. At this stage, ACAS has no power to impose or recommend settlements. ACAS will only agree to conciliate where internal dispute resolution procedures have been exhausted without result. The conciliation process typically involves:

(a) **Fact-finding,** to explore the reasons for the dispute, often through separate meetings of the conciliator with each side.

(b) **Explanation** of each side's position in joint meetings, often facilitated by side meetings between the conciliator and the parties separately, to encourage parties to keep talking and to consider potential areas of movement towards settlement (which parties may not wish to consider openly in full session at first).

(c) **Negotiation** towards a mutually acceptable position, finalised in a joint agreement between the two sides.

If a voluntary settlement is not reached through conciliation, ACAS can arrange for **mediation**. This involves the appointment of an independent person or Board of Mediation, who will consider the case of both sides (set out in writing) and then hear both sides' evidence and arguments at a hearing. The mediator makes a formal proposal or recommendation as a basis for settlement of the dispute, but this is not legally binding on either party.

If both parties agree to **arbitration**:

(a) Terms of reference must be defined, setting limits to the arbitrator's powers and to the issues to be considered.

(b) Parties may select the independent arbitrator from the ACAS panel, or may let ACAS appoint an arbitrator.

(c) A date and venue are set for the arbitration hearing. Prior to the hearing, both sides exchange and submit to the arbitrator a written statement of their case and arguments, supporting documents, and a list of those attending (usually the negotiators). The arbitrator may also request a site visit, for example if the dispute concerns the conditions under which work is done or the level of skill required.

(d) An informal, private and confidential hearing is held, at which the arbitrator hears arguments from both sides. A typical procedure would allow each side an uninterrupted opportunity to state its case and critique the opposing case (as set out in the written submission), prior to questioning by the other side and by the arbitrator. The arbitrator then ensures that both parties have said or asked everything they wish to, and invites closing statements.

(e) The arbitrator considers the arguments after the hearing and delivers an award via ACAS, usually within two to three weeks.

FOR DISCUSSION

Why might employers and trade unions regard arbitration as a little-used instrument of last resort?

What more effective ways might each seek to resolve disputes?

2.3 Conflict resolution

The rationale behind the collaborative approach is explored in the win-win model of conflict resolution. Cornelius and Faire (1989) suggest that there are three basic ways in which a conflict or disagreement can be worked out.

(a) **Win-lose**: one party gets what he wants at the expense of the other party. However well justified such a solution is, there is often lingering resentment on the part of the 'losing' party, which may begin to damage working relationships.

(b) **Lose-lose**: neither party gets what he really wants. Compromise comes into this category. However logical such a solution is, there is often resentment and dissatisfaction on both sides: even positive compromises only result in half-satisfied needs.

(c) **Win-win**: both parties get as close as possible to what they really want. Whether or not such an outcome is possible, the attempt to find it invariably generates more options, more creative and collaborative problem-solving, more open communication and a greater likelihood of preserved working relationships.

A basic win-win approach may be outlined as follows.

(a) **Find out why each party *needs* what they say they *want*.** Probing for, and mapping, both party's fears/concerns and needs in the situation facilitates meaningful problem-solving. It also encourages communication, supports other people's values, and separates the problem from the personalities involved.

(b) **Find out where the differences dovetail.** Diverging needs may seem like the cause of conflict – but they also offer potential for more creative problem-solving, since the different needs may not be mutually exclusive: there may be opportunities for both sets of needs to be satisfied by different means.

(c) **Design more options**, where everyone gets more of what they need. Techniques for doing this include:

   (i) Brainstorming, which temporarily (and by agreement) allows the generation of options temporarily *uncensored* and *uncriticised* by viewpoints which by definition are limited by the conflict;

   (ii) Chunking (breaking a big problem down into manageable chunks and seeking solutions to each); and

   (iii) Devising usable 'currencies' (suggestions and concessions which are easy or low-cost for both parties, and can be traded in negotiation). The aim is *mutual gain*.

(d) **Co-operate**. Treat the other party as a partner in problem-solving, not as an opponent in competition.

EXAMPLE

Dispute resolution procedure: the British Airways walkout

18 July	250 BA staff take part in unofficial walkout after BA announces it is to introduce an electronic swipe-card system.
19 July	Staff return after unions announce talks with BA.
23 July	Talks break down, with unions accusing BA of 'failing to move an inch'.
24 July	GMB and Amicus say that they will ballot staff over strike action.
26 July	Talks resume at conciliation service ACAS after BA chief executive Rod Eddington agrees to attend the talks.
28 July	TUC joins the talks in a 'peace broker' role.
31 July	Unions say the dispute has been resolved, after BA agrees to make scheme voluntary until September, and to separate the issue from ongoing pay negotiations.

(Watkins, 2003 (d))

Activity 3 **(30 minutes)**

From the elements, timetable and result listed in the above example, how successful do you think this dispute resolution was?

2.4 Coping with industrial action

While managerial focus is likely to be on avoiding industrial action, (dispute resolution procedures, threat of sanctions), there should be **contingency plans** in place to minimise the disruptions caused by industrial action if, and when, it occurs.

Depending on the nature of the business, and the group of workers involved, key considerations may be:

(a) **To maintain incoming deliveries** of materials and supplies: eg for a retail organisation, or a factory threatened with picketing

(b) **To maintain production output or service levels**: eg by finding suitable alternative labour (transfers of staff from other sites, or jobs, use of short-contract and casual staff), or re-organising and prioritising (using up existing overstocks, transferring stock from other plans, transferring production to other plants, encouraging overtime working prior to strike)

(c) **To maintain supply of goods and services to the customer**: eg through picket lines, by subcontracting distribution, or encouraging customer self-service.

3 COLLECTIVE BARGAINING

3.1 The nature and scope of collective bargaining

Definition

> **Collective bargaining** is the process whereby employers and employee representatives negotiate agreements by which terms and conditions of employment (and related matters) are determined for groups of represented employees.

Collective bargaining is basically concerned with reaching two types of agreement.

(a) **Substantive agreements**, which determine the terms and conditions of employment. A substantive agreement between a union and employer might cover areas such as: rates of pay for various categories of worker; premium rates of pay; working hours, breaks and holidays; benefits; access to training programmes and so on.

(b) **Procedural agreements**, which determine the methods and procedures for:

(i) Arriving at substantive agreements. (What negotiating machinery should be set up? Should a particular issue be discussed at national level, company level, local plant/branch level – or not at all?)

(ii) Settling any disagreements or disputes which cannot be resolved by normal negotiation. There might be arrangements to refer disputes at plant level to regional or national level, or to arbitration. Procedural rules would determine what the arbitration arrangements should be (eg involving ACAS).

In practice, there are likely to be a range of procedural arrangements and agreements, in areas such as: employee grievances; disciplinary action; redundancy; health and safety; staff development; pay grading; union recognition and so on. Procedural arrangements and agreements basically provide 'law and order' in the workplace: a definition of fair and reasonable behaviour by employers, and the rights and obligations of employees, in a given set of circumstances.

A '**workforce agreement**' is a particular arrangement, under the *Working Time Regulations 1998*, which allows employers to fix working-time arrangements with workers who do not have collectively-agreed terms or conditions. This allows flexibility in taking account of the needs of local workforces or workgroups in applying the regulations.

Note that non-unionised, as well as unionised, organisations have substantive and procedural arrangements (pay grades, dispute procedures etc) in place: employers may (or may not) have drawn these up in consultation with workers.

Gennard & Judge (2003) note that even the outcome of collective bargaining is not, in practice, confined to union members.

(a) Unionised companies apply collectively-bargained terms and conditions to non-union staff as well.

(b) Non-unionised companies partly determine their terms and conditions with regard to market rates – which take into account collectively-bargained terms elsewhere.

3.2 Levels and parties in collective bargaining

Collective bargaining may take place at different levels.

(a) Some issues are discussed at **national (or multi-employer) level**, between *representatives of employers* for the industry or sector and *national trade union officials*. In France, Holland, Italy, Sweden, Finland, Belgium and Spain, for example, sectoral collective agreements are common. These may provide only a basic outline and floor of conditions (for example, minimum rates of pay, maximum weekly and overtime hours, paid holiday entitlements) which trade unions expect to elaborate and improve through company-level agreements.

(b) Other issues will be settled at **company level**, by *representatives of management* and the *unions or staff associations* recognised by the company. Ford, for example, have their own company-wide pay agreements, and do not join in national negotiations with an employers' federation. This allows pay and conditions to be related to the economic and competitive circumstances, and internal equity considerations, of the particular firm.

(c) Other issues will be settled at more local level by '**domestic' (or enterprise) bargaining**, involving representatives of *plant or business unit management* and *local shop stewards*. Phillips Electronics in the UK, for example, has abandoned its national bargaining structure in favour of plant by plant negotiations. This reflects the decentralisation of industrial relations (among other HRM functions) within organisations. Enterprise bargaining may be autonomous, or co-ordinated across all plans/unit, by taking place within centrally-set parameters.

Decentralised bargaining has increased in recent years, because it provides greater flexibility than national agreements. This applies both to the employer (allowing for greater labour flexibility by tailoring work rules and pay agreements to the needs of specific plants) and to the employee (reflecting the desire for more direct influence in employment terms and conditions, which has created a further trend towards individualised contracts). It is also more easily changed, if necessary, because there is less (and more accessible) negotiating machinery. This relative flexibility may have drawbacks, however, if it results in fragmented and inequitable pay structures, inflationary 'leapfrogging' of settlements, and freedom to break or re-negotiate agreements at will. It also relies on competent negotiations by plant-level management.

3.3 Single-table bargaining

Definition

> **Single-table bargaining** describes a situation in which the terms and conditions of all represented workers employed by an establishment are determined in a single set of negotiations. This could involve a single union representing different types and grades of employees (manual and non-manual), or several unions which negotiate a bargaining position amongst themselves prior to negotiating with management as a single bargaining unit.

> **Activity 4** **(45 minutes)**
>
> What would you anticipate to be the advantages and disadvantages of single-table bargaining?

Beardwell and Holden (1997) argue that the significance of single-table bargaining is not primarily its advantages in simplifying and integrating bargaining processes, but the opportunity to extend consultation beyond the basic negotiation forum, to include matters which affect all employees: training and development, fringe benefits, the future direction of the business, change management and so on.

We will be covering employee consultation in Chapter 6, but you should be aware that trade unions recognised for the purpose of collective bargaining are entitled to certain information.

3.4 Disclosure of information

An employer must provide information in response to a written request by a union representative, as long as:

(a) It relates to its (or an associated employer's) undertaking

(b) It is in its possession

(c) It is in accordance with good practice (as laid down in an ACAS Code of Practice)

(d) Lack of the information would materially impede the representative in collective bargaining.

The ACAS Code of Practice recommends that information should be disclosed on pay and benefits, conditions of service, human resources, performance (eg productivity, sales/order forecasts) and financial matters. It suggests that unions should define and request the information before negotiations begin, stating why they consider it relevant.

A union may apply to the Central Arbitration Committee if it believes disclosable information has been withheld. If an employer refuses to comply with a Committee declaration that information should be disclosed, the CAC may make an enforceable award of terms and conditions, at the request of the trade union.

There is no obligation to give information relating to:

(a) Information given in confidence

(b) Information relating to particular individuals

(c) Information which – in any context other than collective bargaining – would cause injury to the undertaking

(d) Information protected by statute (say, in the interests of national security) or subject to legal proceedings.

3.5 Attitudes to collective bargaining

Chamberlain and Kuhn (1965) traced a historical development in attitudes towards collective bargaining.

(a) At first, there was a **marketing theory**, in which collective bargaining was seen as pay bargaining for the supply of labour. Rates of pay would be settled on the basis of supply and demand.

(b) Later, a **governmental (or control) theory** developed. Collective bargaining was seen as a way of making rules of conduct and enforcing those rules in addition to pay bargaining.

(c) Finally, a **managerial theory** emerged, on the basis that decisions about matters in which both management and employees have a vital interest should be discussed and decided by collective negotiation.

A greater range of matters theoretically now come within the sphere of collective bargaining arrangements. Negotiations might cover not only pay, conditions of employment (holidays, hours of work etc) and demarcation lines, but also promotion and training opportunities, fringe benefits, health and safety, equal opportunities and so on. In practice, the Workplace Employee Relations surveys suggest that the number of non-pay items subject to collective bargaining has actually fallen in the private sector.

As we saw in Chapter 16 on union recognition, a managerial approach to collective bargaining is arguably a systematic, efficient, relationship-building and equitable method of conducting industrial relations. It encourages a collectivist orientation which is suited to some cultures of employment and may encourage teamworking and identification with the organisation in others.

Activity 5 **(20 minutes)**

There has been a decline in collective bargaining in recent decades. From what you know of the development of trade unionism during this period, why might this be so?

3.6 The status of collective agreements

In most democratic societies, collective agreements are legally binding: if either party breaks the terms of the agreement, the other can pursue its rights through the courts. This is not the case in the UK! UK collective agreements are only binding in 'honour'. This means that agreements are generally not as comprehensive or precise as legal contracts; they are often reviewed and renegotiated annually. It is, however, important to have rigorous procedural arrangements in place, to define acceptable behaviour and dispute/appeal mechanisms.

4 NEGOTIATION

Definition

> **Negotiation** is a process whereby two parties come together to confer with a view to concluding a jointly acceptable agreement.

4.1 The purpose of negotiation

The general purpose of such a process is for interest groups to attempt to resolve differences between and within themselves, in order to **maintain co-operation** in the pursuit of shared or superordinate goals. Such an approach may be applied in a number of different situations, including collective (and individual) bargaining, conflict resolution and group decision making. Negotiation is basically a **problem-solving technique**, enabling parties to meet their own needs (as far as possible) without breaking the relationship or co-operation between them. This is obviously essential where management and workers are concerned!

Gennard & Judge (2003) suggest that this process requires:

- **Purposeful persuasion**: whereby each party attempts to persuade the other to accept its case by marshalling arguments, backed by factual information and analysis.
- **Constructive compromise**: whereby both parties accept the need to move closer towards each other's position, identifying the parameters of common ground within and between their positions, where there is room for concessions to be made while still meeting the needs of both parties.

Fisher *et al* (1999) suggest three criteria for effective negotiation.

- It should produce a wise agreement: 'one which meets the legitimate interests of each side to the extent possible, resolves conflicting interests fairly, is durable and takes community interests into account'.
- It should be efficient.
- It should improve (or at least not damage) the relationship between the parties.

FOR DISCUSSION

How important is the assumption of on-going relationship in your dealings with other people at work (or in your studies)? What does this encourage you to do, and what does it *prevent* you from doing, in the informal 'negotiations' you conduct every day?

4.2 Approaches to negotiation

There are two approaches to negotiation, which involve different methodologies and outcomes.

(a) **Distributive bargaining**, where negotiation is about the distribution of finite resources. One party's gain is another's loss: a 'win-lose' or 'zero sum' equation. If a pay increase of, say, 10% is gained, where the management budget was 5%, the extra has to be funded from elsewhere – profits, investments, other groups (such as shareholders), increased prices, increased productivity, cuts in training or whatever.

(b) **Integrative bargaining**, based on joint problem-solving, where negotiations aim to find a mutually satisfying solution to problems. This has emerged in recent years in a technique called the 'win-win' approach, a process of exploring and defining the needs and fears of all parties with a view not just to getting the best outcome for one's own party ('win-lose') or even compromise ('lose-lose') but to fulfilling the needs of all parties: a 'win-win' solution may not be available, but the process makes it possible. 'Win-win' negotiation is based on the desire to preserve a constructive relationship between the negotiating parties. 'Win-lose' outcomes can cause resentment or under-motivated performance by the 'losing' party, and perpetuates underlying conflict.

We will be outlining a negotiation process based on concessions and the attempt to find 'middle ground'. However, you should be aware of an alternative approach to collective bargaining, called 'pendulum arbitration'.

Definition

> **Pendulum arbitration** is a system whereby a third party will arbitrate on behalf of the two principals in collective bargaining, should they fail to reach agreement, by awarding the final position of one side or the other: either the employer's final offer or the employees' final claim.

Traditional arbitration draws from both sides of the negotiation in an attempt to find 'middle ground', and this may encourage principals to exaggerate their demands, knowing that they will eventually have to compromise or 'split the difference'. Pendulum arbitration encourages principals to moderate their final positions and to attempt to settle in good faith, knowing that an extreme position will rebound on them if the decision goes to the other side. It avoids the drawing out of the negotiation process by each side holding back from their final position during bargaining.

In practice, however, it is a difficult process, since disputes may involve complex multiple issues, and the final positions of each side on each issue may not be clear.

FOR DISCUSSION

What kind of industrial relations atmosphere is created by a concept such as 'pendulum arbitration'?

Do you think that a 'win-win' solution is possible in collective bargaining?

4.3 The negotiating process

The following (Figure 5.1) is a general overview of the negotiation process. Any negotiation will involve the stages illustrated, although the duration and approach of each will vary according to the particular situation.

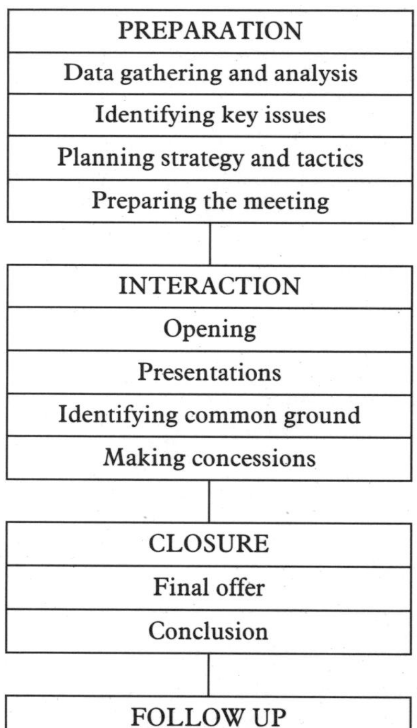

Figure 5.1 The negotiation process

4.4 Preparing a negotiation and negotiation strategy

Formal negotiations, as opposed to informal 'arrangements', should follow broad guidelines.

(a) **Set objectives, parameters and priorities** which are achievable and consistent with industrial relations policy. These are likely to be couched in optimum, most likely and fall-back terms (see (e) below).

(b) **Research the background** of issues over which negotiations are to be conducted: trends in union responses, market pay rates, case studies from similar organisations/sectors, relevant legislation and court decisions and so on.

(c) **Recognise potential for conflict.** In an integrative framework, each side accepts that the objectives and perspectives of the other side are as genuine and legitimate as their own. Even in a distributive framework, it must be recognised that the outcome will have to be 'sold' to all parties, and the consequences of resistance, resentment and lost relationship managed. Recognition of the needs, wants and fears of the other party helps in managing expectations and in the process of devising a workable trade-off between divergent interests.

(d) **Identify tradable items and bargaining power**. Each party identifies the key issues or items likely to be on the bargaining agenda, and decides on which of these it will be willing to trade or make concessions. It also tries to anticipate the items on which the other party will be willing to trade or make concessions. Some items will be non-tradable: others may be amenable to movement on both sides, especially if some items are identified as being relatively 'cheap' for one party to give up and relatively valuable for the other party to receive.

Each party may also attempt to evaluate its bargaining power, relative to the other party. A frequently used formula for this is:

$$\text{Bargaining power of A} = \frac{\text{Costs to B of disagreement with A's terms}}{\text{Costs to A of disagreement with B's terms}}$$

If the cost of disagreeing is greater than the cost of agreeing, the bargaining power lies with the other side.

Activity 6 **(10 minutes)**

This bargaining power model provides a quantitative measure of relative bargaining power. What other, more qualitative factors are there that might enhance or detract from the bargaining power of one side or the other?

(e) **Determine negotiating strategy**. Given a fair idea of what the other side's position and bargaining power are likely to be, the party in question should be able to predict any demands the other side will make, or what kind of offer is likely to be accepted. Each side should look for potential counter-arguments to its own case, without underestimating the potential gap between the parties.

There are basically three possible outcomes for either side:

(i) If we were to achieve all our objectives, what would be the *ideal settlement* or outcome?

(ii) If we were to make progress, but being realistic about the power of the other side, what is a *realistic settlement* or outcome?

(iii) If we were to concede, what is an acceptable *fall-back position*: the least favourable outcome that can be accepted without failing to meet our objectives?

A position for each side should be estimated for each of the above situations, and areas of agreement concentrated on, as potential *middle ground*.

John Sawbridge (*People Management* 14 September 2000) suggests that a union will 'move' (make concessions) only if it believes that: there is no other option; its members will benefit; and it will be painful not to do so.

(f) **Determine the agenda** ('terms of reference') of the meeting. The agenda for negotiation should be accepted (or acceptable) in advance by both sides. The order of items may have tactical significance: imposing time pressures for agreement on issues raised late in the day, say, or gaining momentum on related issues by placing them after a major point of agreement.

(g) **Issue prior information**. This may be done:

(i) As pre-conditioning: for example, advance announcement of poor trading results and intense competition as a prelude to negotiating pay awards, redundancies or productivity agreements.

(ii) As a matter of legal obligation. Information relevant to collective bargaining must be disclosed to trade union representatives (see above).

(iii) To allow all parties to do their homework, for better quality decision-making, (unless there is any assumed advantage in surprise disclosures).

(h) **Select participants.** Representatives of management must be articulate, persuasive, acceptable to employee representatives and authoritative enough to implement agreed decisions. Face-to-face negotiations require particular skills in persuasion, personal rapport, reading of verbal and non-verbal signals and so on.

4.5 Conduct of negotiation

During the conduct of the negotiations themselves, participants should consider the following.

(a) **Opening presentation**: a broad statement of each side's ideal position or opening offer, explaining the rationale (and strength of feeling) behind the proposals and supporting them with relevant data. This will be a clue to strategy – and may also be an opportunity for broad general agreement. It is recommended that the party seeking change be invited to state its case first.

(b) **Fact-finding**: each party should use the other party's presentation as an opportunity for fact-finding, rather than point scoring or unconsidered ('knee-jerk') opposition. Active listening should be used to clarify or expand on proposals, or to probe for supporting data. During the fact-finding process, the negotiator should gain a better understanding of the other party's ideal position or proposal *and* its strengths and weaknesses (Dobler *et al*, 1990). At the end of this session, there may be a recess or adjournment to allow negotiators to reassess their positions and strategies.

(c) **Identifying common ground**: having established each others' ideal positions (potentially polarised differences) the emphasis switches to exploring the territory *within* the bargaining range in which agreement might be reached; the room for manoeuvre offered by both parties' (possibly dovetailed) realistic and fall-back positions should be explored.

(d) **Use of the negotiating strategy and bargaining power**. Items should be linked and packaged to achieve two-way momentum, so that no party gives away anything without getting something in return. Be firm on principles and flexible on details, so that there is room to move without compromising strategic priorities.

(e) **Making concessions**. A concession is 'a revision of a position you have held previously and justified publicly' (Guirdham, 1995). Concessions are not easy to make without undermining credibility – but *must* be made in order to bring both parties progressively closer together. They should be made only in response to pressure – or to offers-in-exchange from the other party – and in small increments. **Reciprocal concessions** can be promoted by negatively reinforcing the other side's present position (eg emphasising that it will not work) and positively reinforcing movement (eg offering options for them to move without losing face).

The meeting should be facilitated by an experienced chairperson, who will ensure that the meeting is conducted in a courteous and effective manner: sticking to the point of the agenda reached; giving alternating opportunities to speak (rather than a 'free for all'); and so on.

Activity 7 **(30 minutes)**

From your study or awareness of communication and persuasion techniques, suggest some techniques which you might use in negotiation.

Adjournments may be used to give parties time to review progress, consider proposals, enter informal 'off-the-table' discussions which might help break an impasse, or just 'cool off' when negotiation reaches a heated stage.

All relevant details of the discussion should be recorded by a minute-taker, stenographer or sound recorder, in order to furnish minutes which can be used in formulating final agreements.

4.6 Settlement and follow-up

At the conclusion of negotiations, both parties must be satisfied that all issues have been discussed and that they understand exactly what has been agreed: the proceedings should be summarised and agreements 'played back' for confirmation by both sides. If there is any misunderstanding or ambiguity which raises objections, negotiations should recommence.

Once there is oral agreement, the points should be written up as a signed 'draft agreement', stating:

(a) Who made the agreement and on what date

(b) Who is to be covered by the agreement (groups and grades of employee, for example)

(c) When the agreement is to take effect, how long it is to run, and whether and how it may be amended or terminated prior to this date

(d) The contents (or 'clauses') of the agreement and any exceptions that may apply

(e) How disagreements and appeals will be dealt with once the negotiated settlement is implemented.

The draft agreement should be circulated and checked by both sides, and clauses initialled once their wording is accepted. When all clauses have been approved by both sides, the agreement can be printed, formally signed and communicated to those affected by its provisions.

Activity 8 **(1 hour)**

In an example cited by Gennard and Judge (2003), the annual pay negotiations between a trade union and a manufacturing company started with the following sets of demands.

Trade Union

- Substantial increase on all basic rates of pay
- Holiday pay to be improved, to include all earnings in the 12 weeks prior to the holiday period
- Shift premiums payable at weekends to be raised to double-time and for nightwork to time-and-a-third
- Overtime payments to be time-and-a-half (standard) and double-time plus time in lieu (customary holidays)
- Drivers' overnight allowance increased to £20 per occasion

Manufacturer

- Wage increase of 1.5%
- No changes to the basis of calculation of holiday pay
- No changes to shift premiums
- No changes to overtime payments
- Drivers' overnight allowance increased to £18 per occasion
- Any additional costs of the settlement to be recovered in full by efficiency and productivity improvements at plant levels

Consider which items are most important, and which most tradable, for each side. (If possible, role play a negotiation with a fellow student.) Come up with a 'trade' of terms that you think might be acceptable to both parties.

Chapter roundup

- A lawful trade dispute is one between workers and their own employers, wholly or mainly about work-related matters. Various forms of sanctions are available to workers in pursuance of an industrial dispute, including strikes. Strike action has been strictly controlled by legislation and has correspondingly declined in severity and frequency.
- Collective bargaining is the process whereby employee and employer representatives negotiate agreements on terms and conditions of employment (and related matters) for groups of represented employees. There has been a tendency to decentralise bargaining to plant level, in order to retain flexibility.
- Negotiating is a bargaining process through which commitments and compromises are reached, using the relative power of the parties involved.

Quick quiz

1 Distinguish between primary and secondary industrial action.

2 List five areas of industrial action that are subject to UK legislation.

3 Outline the process of arbitration of a trade dispute and the role of ACAS.

4 What are procedural agreements in collective bargaining?

5 What is single-table bargaining?

6 What does the ACAS Code of Practice recommend on the disclosure of information for collective bargaining?

7 What is pendulum arbitration?

8 What three outcomes of negotiation should negotiators plan in advance, as the basis of negotiating strategy?

9 What is the 'win-win' approach?

10 Draw an overview of the process of negotiation.

Answers to quick quiz

1 Primary: aimed at the employer with whom the participating union is in dispute. Secondary (unlawful): aimed at employers who trade with firms in dispute. (para 1.2)

2 Balloting of members; legal immunity for lawful dispute; outlawing of secondary action; individual member rights not to participate; unlawful dismissal of strikers in first eight weeks of dispute. (para 1.4)

3 See paragraph 2.2 for a full answer.

4 Agreements which determine methods and procedures for arriving at substantive agreements (on pay, conditions and so on) and for settling disputes. (para 3.1)

5 Terms and conditions of all workers (manual and non-manual) are determined in a single negotiation. This may be achieved by multiple unions pre-

negotiating a bargaining proposal prior to collective bargaining with management. (para 3.3)

6 Information should be disclosed on pay and benefits, conditions of service, human resources, performance (productivity, sales, orders) and financial matters. Unions should define and request specific information before negotiations begin. (para 3.4)

7 Instead of the arbitrator finding 'middle ground' between the final offer/claim of each side, (s)he awards for one side's final position over the other: **either** the employer's final offer **or** the employees' final claim. (para 4.2)

8 Ideal settlement, realistic settlement, fall-back position. (para 4.4)

9 An approach to conflict resolution and distributive bargaining/negotiation which seeks to meet the needs of both parties as far as possible. (paras 2.3, 4.2)

10 See paragraph 4.3 (Figure 5.1).

Answers to activities

1 Industrial action may be used as:

(a) A demonstration of bargaining strength, by the threatened or actual withdrawal of labour and/or restriction of productivity, aimed at forcing management to enter negotiations or make concessions, or

(b) A gesture of protest to highlight a grievance issue, aimed at management, government and other influential bodies, or at the general public. (For example, a literal 'go-slow' was staged by a transport union in Sydney, Australia in November 2000. Bus drivers drove at a crawl during the rush hour to highlight the failure of state government and policy to enforce city-centre bus lane rules, exposing drivers to stress, risk and commuter frustration: passengers and the media were handed leaflets explaining the purpose of the action and urged to support the protest.)

2 The main industrial sanctions available to the *employer* are:

- Locking out some, or all, of the workforce from the worksite
- Closing the worksite and/or relocating operations elsewhere
- Dismissing employees who participate in industrial action

The main reasons why these are 'last resort measures' is because:

(a) They are costly, involving lost production/service. Without alternative arrangements this may mean lost orders and lost customers.

(b) They risk escalating the conflict, hardening attitudes on both sides.

(c) They risk long-term damage to the loyalty and commitment of staff after the particular dispute is over.

(d) They need to be carefully checked for legality, with regard to detail (eg if it is unlawful to dismiss within the first eight weeks of a strike).

3 The dispute was effectively resolved within two weeks.

The unions successfully got together to bring staff to the discussion table with BA initially, and persuaded them to return to work on this basis.

First-round talks appear not to have been successful. However, this may have been a bargaining strategy by BA, determined not to give way initially, given the unofficial nature of the original worker action. Positive use is made of third-party conciliation, both through ACAS and the TUC.

The involvement of the chief executive is a positive gesture of willingness by BA to come to the table seriously.

The outcome is relatively satisfactory to both sides. It appears that the swipe-card system may in itself be not the prime cause of the dispute, but worker fears about the erosion of their flexible working arrangements (work-life balance), lack of managerial trust and so on. The procedure will only have been truly successful insofar as these matters were brought into the open and discussed.

4 **Advantages**

(a) Less time and resources spent on negotiations than with multiple bargaining.

(b) Takes account of more viewpoints, more representative: enhances likelihood of acceptance of decisions. (Particularly helpful for change management affecting multiple groups of employees.)

(c) Encourages resolution of inter-union disputes as part of preparation for negotiation: saves wasted time and energy in harmonising separate agreements.

(d) May help avoid demarcations and inflexible work rules, with overall bargaining perspective (needs for flexibility, quality etc).

Disadvantages

(a) Agenda may be overcrowded by concerns of multiple groups.

(b) Requires higher levels of negotiating and relationship management skills.

(c) Inflexibility: management may be less able to differentiate and change agreements with different segments of the workforce.

(d) Inter-union disputes may not be resolved prior to negotiation.

(e) May hamper individual union attempts to recruit members.

5 Decline in collective bargaining, due to:

(a) The decline in union membership, and therefore the number of workers covered by collective bargaining

(b) The rise of individual– and team-based systems, with new emphasis on employees' responsibility for self-management and self-development: individual contracts, learning plans and career mobility; team-centred performance management, performance-related pay and so on

(c) The rise of workforce flexibility, with the erosion of job descriptions, occupational demarcations and associated work rules

(d) The decentralisation of employee relations (and other HRM) processes to line managers

(e) The introduction of non-negotiatory consultation and involvement techniques

As we saw in Chapter 4, however, union recognition in the UK may be on the upturn: watch this space!

6 Quantitative elements of bargaining power include:

- The intrinsic merit of each party's case or argument (the stronger your case, the better the prospect of achieving agreement on your terms)
- The skill and ability of the negotiator
- The potential for coercion (the power of underlying sanctions or 'threat' eg to close a plant, or initiate industrial action)

Note that bargaining power may be actual or 'real' and/or perceived, and that the one may be much higher or lower than the other…

7 (a) Gain agreements or commitments from the other side that can be used as a stepping stone for the logical progression of your argument.

(b) Summarise periodically, especially to highlight common ground and consolidate progress.

(c) Sell the benefits of your proposals to the other side: allow them to agree with you, without loss of face, whenever possible.

(d) Preserve a tone of commitment, belief, even emotion: make your cause human.

(e) Use questions. Positive, joint-problem-solving questions: 'What would it take to make this work?'. Probing, challenging questions: 'Where would the money for that proposal come from?' Push for answers where necessary.

(f) Release information with a tactical awareness of its affects on negotiating position.

(g) Use all interpersonal and communication skills: listening, empathy, accessible language, giving non-verbal cues (eg confident body-language) and interpreting non-verbal cues (eg signs of hesitation, tentative phrasing, suggestions of readiness to move).

8 In the example cited, the agreed settlement was as follows.

Company conceded	*Company gained*
• Wage increase of 1.5%	• No changes to holiday pay
• Increase in drivers' overnight allowance to £20 per occasion	• No change to weekend shift premiums
• Shiftwork premiums (nightwork) increased to time-and-a-third	• No change to overtime premiums
	• Additional costs of the agreement fully covered by efficiency/productivity improvements

Chapter 6:

EMPLOYEE PARTICIPATION AND INVOLVEMENT

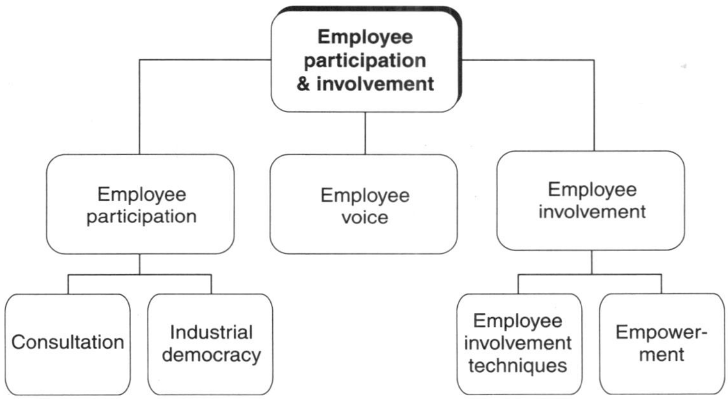

Introduction

The concept of 'employee voice' embraces 'a whole variety of processes and structures which enable, and sometimes empower employees, directly and indirectly, to contribute to decision-making in the firm' (Boxall & Purcell, 2003). The term has come to embrace a wide range of mechanisms for:

- **Employee involvement**: informing and consulting employees about aspects of decision making
- **Employee participation**: involving employees (often via their representatives) in the decision making machinery of the organisation.

In this chapter, we look at both of these key aspects of employee relations, exploring the role of HRM and line management in shifting focus **from 'industrial relations' to 'employee relations'**, and from a unitarist towards a pluralist frame of reference.

Your objectives

In this chapter you will learn about the following.

(a) Different forms of employee consultation and participation

(b) Industrial democracy and its European roots

(c) Employee involvement techniques

(d) Empowerment

(e) Employee voice

1 EMPLOYEE VOICE

1.1 What is employee voice?

Armstrong (2009) summarises 'employee voice' as 'the say employees have in matters of concern to them in their organisation'. He suggests that this is closer to **participation** ('ensuring that employees are given the opportunity to influence management decisions and to contribute to the improvement of organisations performance') than to **involvement** (where 'management allows employees to discuss with it issues that affect them, but management retains the right to manage'). However, employee voice may be seen as a framework for both processes.

Employee voice is both an individual concept and a collective concept: it includes, for example, individual grievances and suggestions as well as collective bargaining and industrial democracy agreements made with trade unions and/or other employee representatives.

Marchington *et al* (2001) model the territory of employee voice as follows: Figure 6.1.

(a) Involvement may be **direct** (where management deal with individuals/ teams) or **indirect** (where management deal with trade unions or other representative groups)

(b) Involvement may be based on a **shared agenda** (directed at improving organisational performance and the quality of working life) or on a **contested agenda** (directed at addressing areas of conflict, dissatisfaction or competition).

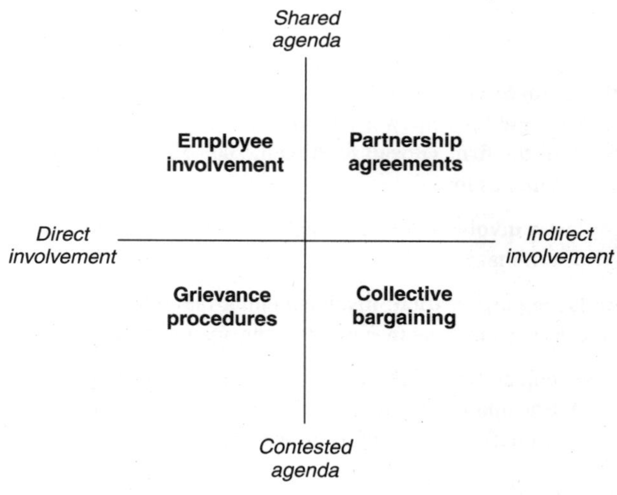

Figure 6.1: Employee voice matrix

In practice, an organisation's approach will be a mixture of direct and indirect, and focus on both shared and contested agendas (weighted according to whether HRM policies take a pluralistic or unitarist viewpoint, as discussed in Chapter 4). If there is an anti-union culture of management, the balance will shift towards direct involvement. If there is a co-operative or unitarist culture of management, the balance will shift towards shared agenda.

1.2 Purposes of employee voice

Marchington *et al* (2001) suggest that employee voice offers:

(a) The ability for individual employees to express dissatisfaction, solve problems with management and preserve working relationships

(b) The ability for employees collectively to express their needs and wishes in matters that affect them, providing a counterbalance to managerial power

(c) The ability for employees to contribute to management decisions, allowing the organisation to harness the expertise and commitment of workers to improve quality, productivity and work organisation

(d) The ability for employers and employees to demonstrate their intention to focus on shared goals, mutual interests and co-operative working relations, for the long-term benefit of the organisation and its people.

Employee voice thus involves both 'soft' HRM elements (fairness, relationship, mutual commitment) and 'hard' HRM elements (problem-solving, conflict/grievance management and performance improvement).

1.3 Mechanisms of employee voice

Marchington *et al* (1992, 2001) classify the main approaches to implementing employee voice as 'representative participation' (which we call 'participation' in this chapter) and 'upward problem-solving' (which we include among techniques for 'involvement').

(a) **Representative participation** includes:

(i) **Collective representation**: grievance procedures, collective bargaining, collective dispute resolution and other settings in which trade unions, staff associations or elected employee representatives represent the interests of individual employees or groups of employees (as discussed in Chapters 4-5).

(ii) **Joint consultation**: formal non-negotiatory meetings between management and employee representatives to discuss matters of shared interest or concern (discussed in Section 2 below).

(iii) **European Works Councils**: joint consultation machinery for organisations with sites in two or more member states of the European Union (discussed in Section 2 below).

(iv) **Partnership schemes**: formal agreements between management and employee representatives to work together for mutual benefit, in a non-adversarial climate (discussed in Section 2 below).

(b) **Upward problem-solving** includes:

(i) **Two-way communication**: encouraging upward communication (from staff to management) as well as downward, eg through briefing groups, team meetings and corporate intranets.

(ii) **Upward communication**: seeking staff feedback, opinions and suggestions, eg through attitude surveys, suggestion schemes and employee intranet discussion groups.

(iii) **Project teams**: getting staff and management together to solve problems, discuss issues or generate ideas (eg quality circles, customer care task forces).

FOR DISCUSSION

'What institution embodying the employee voice might be appropriate? Is it a trade union? A works council? Or should employee voice not be viewed any longer in terms of collective representation?' (Gennard & Judge, 2003)

What do you think?

We will now go on to look at some of the mechanisms of employee voice in more detail.

2 EMPLOYEE PARTICIPATION AND CONSULTATION

2.1 What is participation?

Definition

> **Employee participation** 'concerns the extent to which employees, often via their representatives, are involved in the decision-making machinery of the organisation. This includes joint consultation, collective bargaining and worker representation on the board' (Gennard & Judge, 2003).

As noted in Section 1, there are different degrees and methods of participation, reflecting the extent to which organisations wish to involve employees in decision-making.

> **Activity 1** **(30 minutes)**
>
> Outline four general reasons why an organisation may consider it desirable or necessary to work towards employee participation.

2.2 Information and consultation

Some of the circumstances in which recognised trade unions (or other employee representatives) are legally entitled to information and consultation, include:

- **Redundancy**, where more than 20 people are affected
- **Health and safety**
- **Collective bargaining** (see Chapter 5)

Redundancy and health and safety are covered in the Human Resources Management Course book.

FOR DISCUSSION

The general secretary of the GMB told the 2000 TUC conference: 'We need better rights to consultation and information. I look forward to the day when British workers hear about the changes in their employment from the lips of their managers and not from the pages of the *Financial Times* or the early morning news bulletins of the BBC'.

Do workers have a 'right' to information and consultation in a moral sense?

Consultation, from a legal point of view, means talking formally to employee representatives on a matter which will affect employees or their work, with a view to seeking agreement. There is no obligation on employers to negotiate or take employee views into account in any specific way – but there must be dialogue entered into 'in good faith'.

Under the Companies Act 1989, an organisation employing more than 250 employees is required to include a statement in its Directors' Report describing the action taken in the previous financial year to introduce, maintain or develop arrangements for:

(a) Information/consultation of employees on matters affecting their employment

(b) Consultation with employee representatives to canvass their views on matters affecting them

(c) Financial participation of employees in the company's performance

(d) Extending employees' awareness of financial and economic factors affecting the company's performance.

Activity 2 **(no time limit)**

Get hold of the Directors' Report (found as part of the Annual Report and Accounts) of any public limited company of your choice. Examine the statements made in regard to the above matters. Do they reflect genuine involvement or participation, from what you can gather?

2.3 Joint consultation and works councils

Definition

Joint consultation is a process by which management and employee representatives jointly examine and discuss issues of mutual concern.

Joint consultation is the main form of representative participation in the UK. Gennard and Judge (2003) distinguish between 'employee communication' (similarly concerned with the interchange of information and ideas within an organisation) and 'consultation', which involves managers actively seeking and taking account of the views of employees before making a decision. Consultation 'affects the process through which decisions are made in so far as it commits management first to the **disclosure of information** at an early stage in the decision-making process and second to take into account the **collective views** of the employees.'

Joint Consultative Committees (JCCs) – sometimes called **'Works Councils'** – are composed of managers and employee representatives who come together on a regular basis to discuss matters of mutual interest. Members should include senior managers (in order to demonstrate commitment and mobilise authority where required) and representatives of all significant employee groups (in order to be regarded as genuinely representative). Committees usually have a well defined constitution and terms of reference.

Like any committee or group meeting, a JCC meeting will need a skilled Chairperson to facilitate and control discussion, and a clear and manageable agenda, circulated in advance for member preparation. Minutes will need to be taken for feeding back to the parties represented (via briefing groups, noticeboards, intranet and so on). Management needs to demonstrate its commitment to genuine consultation by giving appropriate facilities, time off and training to committee members. In unionised organisations, issues such as pay bargaining are generally left to collective bargaining, so JCCs must also be given something of perceived importance to deal with if they are not to be marginalised as ineffectual 'talk shops'.

Activity 3 **(no time limit)**

What are the structures for joint consultation in your work organisation (or one you know well or can find out about). What issues are consultations designed to cover? What influence do they have on organisational policy? How are they regarded by employees in general?

Bratton & Gold (2007) suggest that there are arguments both for **integrating** consultative machinery with negotiating (collective bargaining) machinery in an organisation and for **separating** the two activities.

Arguments for integration	Arguments for separation
• Communicating, consulting and negotiation are interlinked processes • Union reps must be involved in consultation anyway • As collective bargaining's scope expands, remaining issues are less important	• May reduce organisational complexity • Collective bargaining deals with substantive/procedural matters: consultation addresses other matters • Regular JCC meetings ensure that consultation is (and is seen to be) a managerial commitment

2.4 European Works Councils

While JCCs are voluntary works councils, the term 'European Works Council' is specifically used to describe mandatory meetings between management and elected employee representatives (independent of trade unions) under the European Works

Council Directive, which became law in the UK as the Transnational Information and Consultation of Employees Regulations 1999.

A **European Works Council** must be set up in all organisations with more than 1,000 employees in Member States and employing more than 150 people in each of two or more of these. A **Pan-European Works Council** (or alternative) has to be agreed between central management and a Special Negotiating Body of employee representatives from the countries involved.

If no agreement is reached, a fallback system requires the establishment of a **European Works Council** of employee representatives with the right to meet central management at least once a year for information and consultation about the progress and prospects of the company. It may also request further or special meetings on transnational ('community scale') issues of concern, defined as 'measures significantly affecting employees' interests': large scale redundancies, for example.

EXAMPLE

Electrics giant Panasonic decided in 1994 to adopt a proactive view of the European Works Council Directive and to conclude a voluntary agreement with employee representatives, resulting in the establishment of:

(a) A 'Panasonic European Congress' (PEC), meeting yearly for consultation on transnational issues. The congress involves representatives from different nations; different types of operations (sales, manufacturing, R & D) and both unionised and non-unionised companies.

(b) Two representative committees: an Employee Representative Committee and a Management Representative Committee, which meet three or four times a year to discuss the agenda for the annual meeting, agree the minutes and be informed and consulted on transnational issues.

(c) A Panasonic UK Consultative Committee (PUCC), with 11 employee representatives from the different divisions of Panasonic UK Ltd. (The UK company was non-union and non-works-council, so there was no existing formal structure for information and consultation with elected employee representatives.) The PUCC meets with company directors every two months to discuss company performance, sales figures, health and safety, canteen and sports facilities, technological and structural changes and training and education.

Note that EWCs do not represent industrial democracy or co-determination such as operates in countries such as Germany or Sweden (discussed later in this section). They are only for the purposes of consultation.

(a) Councils have the right to be informed and consulted about 'any measure likely to have a considerable effect on employees' interests'.

(b) Matters for discussion must be transnational or 'community scale': this is not an alternative forum to discuss matters affecting a single group of employees.

The original EWC Directive was replaced by the recast EWC Directive in April 2009.

FOR DISCUSSION

Running costs for an EWC have been reported as running as high as £150,000 a year, because of training, travel and transportation costs, and the entitlement to 'assistance' from an expert paid for by the employer.

How might developments in Information and Communications Technology (ICT) be used to reduce the cost of meetings – and/or keep the wider employee body better informed in general?

2.5 Information and Consultation of Employees Regulations 2004

Under the ICE Regulations employers must:

(a) Inform representatives about recent and foreseeable developments concerning the enterprise's activity and economic and financial situation

(b) Consult representatives on any restructuring of employment (particularly, threat to jobs) with a view to exchanging views

(c) Consult representatives on decisions that are likely to lead to substantial changes in work organisation and contractual relations (eg collective redundancies or business transfers) 'with a view to reaching agreement'.

The practical arrangements used for information and consultation must be agreed by the workforce. If current structures do not meet the requirements of the Regulations, management will have to negotiate new machinery with employee representatives. The procedures may be triggered by a formal request from employees or by the initiative of the employer.

Since April 2008, the ICE provisions have applied to businesses with 50 or more employees.

EXAMPLE

In 2003, 13 people from all walks of life and all levels of Marks & Spencer participated in the first meeting of its national business involvement group (Big), the company's body for information and consultation. Their role was to debate business decisions and HR policies face-to-face with their chief executive.

These types of staff council are being established in companies across the UK in response to the European directive on information and consultation… But for M&S, the new group was the culmination of a series of measures aimed at improving employee communications.

There have been discussion groups in the stores for some years. But during the firm's financial difficulties in 1999, staff were involved in a consultative process called Clearview, which moved communications up a gear. It involved brainstorming sessions between employees and managers to consider what was wrong with the structure, processes and culture of the business.

M&S recognised the contribution that such a process made to the organisation's recovery. A review of the staff focus groups in Spring 2001 indicated that they wanted a structure that enabled issues to be represented at a more senior level and wanted managers and staff to sit in a combined forum. This led to the creation of Bigs at a local and area level in September 2001.

Local Bigs were set up in 309 shops, head office locations, the financial services unit and its distribution centres. Area Bigs provided a forum for issues that affected more than one store or business area. The company also had a European council, established in 1995 in line with EU legislation. But discussions were confined to issues affecting more than two countries. This was despite the closure of continental European stores in 2001, leaving the European council with members from only the UK and the Republic of Ireland. A review in March 2002 highlighted the need for a national forum.

(Higginbottom, 2003 (c))

2.6 Information and consultation: summary

The following (Figure 6.2) is a helpful schematic showing various methods of employee information and consultation (*source unknown*).

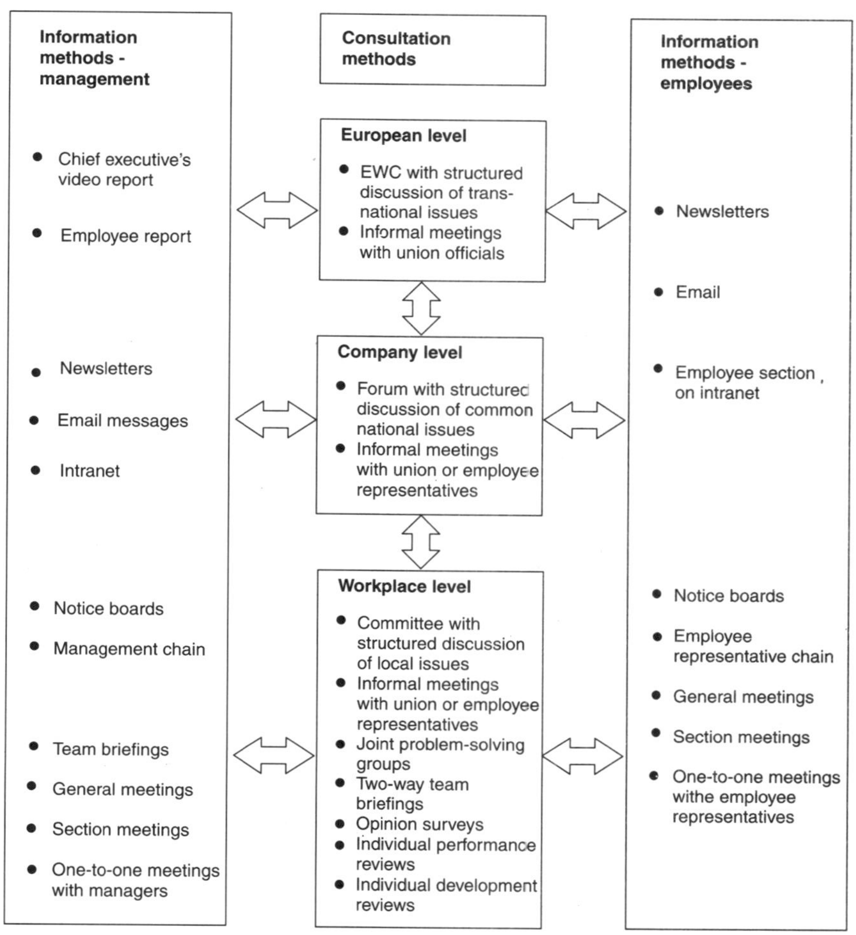

Figure 6.2: An information and consultation structure

Weblinks

- CIPD *(2009 Factsheet on Employee Voice)*

▶▶ **http://www.cipd.co.uk/subjects/empreltns/comconsult**

- CIPD *(2009 Factsheet on European Works Councils)*

▶▶ **http://www.cipd.co.uk/subjects/empreltns/workcncls**

2.7 Partnership agreements

Definition

Partnership agreements are negotiated arrangements 'in which both parties (management and the trade union) agree to work together to their mutual advantage and to achieve a climate of more co-operative and therefore less adversarial industrial relations.' (Armstrong, 2003)

Partnership agreements generally include undertakings from both sides, linking job security, pay awards or participation (in the control of management) to productivity gains or greater flexibility in work organisation (in the control of unions).

Gennard & Judge (2003) identify six key principles underpinning partnership agreements in the workplace.

Principle		Comment
1	Commitment to success of the enterprise	Partnership depends on shared understanding and commitment in regard to the business goals of the organisation
2	Recognising legitimate interests	A recognition that interests and priorities will not always coincide: parties must respect each others' responsibility to do their best for their stakeholders
3	Commitment to employment security	Measures to maximise employment security (eg limit redundancies) and improve staff employability (eg through transferable skills training)
4	Focus on the quality of working life	Recognition of the need to develop employees and create opportunities for personal growth
5	Transparency	Real sharing of information and early discussion of plans for the future
6	Adding value	Partnership should access and deploy commitment/resources not available through previous employee relations machinery

Activity 4 **(30 minutes)**

What advantages might parties in a partnership agreement be aiming for?

Note that partnership also has its critics!

> There are critics who see partnership as an illusory concept. Those on the left of the political spectrum... fear that unions, far from gaining influence, will be co-opted by management into their projects, effectively neutralising any chance of opposition. Critics from the right would argue that partnership hampers management's ability to manage, or, as the president of the CBI... believes, that it may even provide a 'Trojan horse' through which unions could gain more influence.
>
> (*People Management*, 14 September 2000)

We will now look briefly at European models of employee participation, which are closer to 'industrial democracy'.

3 EMPLOYEE PARTICIPATION AND INDUSTRIAL DEMOCRACY

3.1 Social dimensions of the European Union

The European Union was partly developed as a 'Single Market' or trading bloc, removing barriers to trade and competitive bias, standardising technical regulations and creating a convergence of conditions between European markets. However, it also has a socio-political dimension which embraces employment issues, since it is believed that the success of the Single Market depends on the united efforts of employers and labour.

The main statement of European social policy is the 'Community Charter of the Fundamental Social Rights of Workers'– commonly known as the 'Social Charter' – which was ratified by 11 of the (then) 12 member states: the UK opted out. The Charter is based on the desire to improve living and working conditions and to ensure effective use of human resources across the EU. It is a statement of intent to guarantee individual rights in areas such as: freedom of movement; fair remuneration; improvement of living and working conditions (including working time); freedom of association and collective bargaining (the right to join, or not to join, a trade union; the right to negotiate and conclude collective agreements and the right to collective action such as strikes); access to vocational training; equal treatment for men and women; health and safety in the workplace; and the protection of children, adolescents and the disabled in the workplace.

Additional rights are guaranteed in respect of the information, consultation and participation of workers. Changes that affect the workforce such as new technology, working practices, mergers, restructuring and collective redundancy should involve prior consultation with employees.

All members of the EU have since agreed that the Social Charter be implemented by directive: member states will be bound to legislate and 'mobilise all the resources necessary' to implement its provisions. Some have already been covered by EU Directives, while others are still subject to negotiation and amendment.

3.2 The European Company Statute

The European Public Limited-Liability Company Regulations 2004 give companies the option of forming a European company which can operate on a Europe-wide basis and be governed by Community law. An accompanying Directive requires employee involvement arrangements in all such companies, including:

(a) Collective bargaining on decisions or

(b) A two-tier board structure, with elected worker representatives on the senior or 'supervisory' board to which the management or 'executive' board is responsible, or

(c) A unitary board structure with worker representatives as non-executive directors, or

(d) A sub-board level company council, solely comprised of worker representation.

3.3 National cultural differences in regard to participation

In **Germany**, the concept of consultation and participation is based on a system called **co-determination**, formally involving employees and their representatives in nearly all decisions relating to personnel and other aspects of company policy. Co-determination is supported by specific legislation. There are three methods by which workers can participate: by Works Councils, Supervisory Boards and Management Boards.

(a) In workplaces with more than five employees, the workforce elects a **works council** consisting solely of workers' representatives. This council has the right:

   (i) To receive information on health and safety, work organisation, jobs, work environment, the hiring of executives and planned changes which could adversely affect employees

   (ii) To make suggestions during the formulation and implementation of HR plans, and specifically regarding vocational training (eg apprenticeships) and other training and development opportunities.

   The views and suggestions of the council must be considered, although they are not binding on managerial decision-making.

(b) In companies employing more than 500 people, elected worker representatives sit on the **supervisory board** which meets four times a year. Worker representatives make up one-third to one-half of this policy-making body (depending on size), with other board members elected by the shareholders, under a 'neutral' chairperson. The supervisory board is responsible for deciding the overall direction of the enterprise; matters concerning corporate finance and structure (including mergers and takeovers); and the appointment, dismissal and remuneration of members of the executive or management board.

(c) The executive or **management board** is the full-time body responsible for the day-to-day running of operations.

Sweden also operates a co-determination system based on consultation with employees and the participation of representatives in decision making at both board and shop floor levels. Industrial democracy was developed early in Sweden, and techniques such as job enrichment, autonomous working groups and 'quality of working life' programmes were developed by companies such as Volvo back in the 1970s. The Swedish model is more highly unionised that the German model, with union membership over 80%.

Belgium, France, Italy, Spain and the Netherlands also have works councils supported by legislation, but the range of issues open to employee approval is smaller than in the German or Swedish co-determination models. Belgium and the Netherlands have an additional legal requirement for large companies to operate a two-tier (supervisory and executive) board of directors.

In **Japan**, employee involvement practices are deeply embedded in the collectivist and commitment-based culture of employment, in techniques such as quality circles, teamworking, consensus decision-making and long-term employee development. There is a unitarist assumption of the value of participation, supported by the training of group leaders and workers in the skills of participative working. However, observers note that employee involvement techniques are not primarily used as decision-making mechanisms or channels of communication (as in Europe) but as a cultural mechanism reinforcing identification with shared aims and goals.

Activity 5 **(5 minutes)**

From your knowledge of national cultural differences (For example, your studies from the Human Resources Management Course Book) what characteristics would you expect to be most relevant to a country's acceptance of industrial democracy?

As you read through the next section, bear in mind the issues of reward, quality management, flexibility and development. These form part of the overall relationship between employees and management.

4 EMPLOYEE INVOLVEMENT TECHNIQUES

4.1 Employee involvement

Definition

Employee involvement describes a wide range of policies and techniques for 'informing and consulting employees about, or associating them with, one or more aspects of running an organisation.' (Gennard & Judge, 2003)

Employee involvement concentrates mainly on individual employees and the degree to which they can be encouraged to identify with the goals of the organisation. It can be distinguished from employee participation (discussed earlier), which concerns the extent to which employees are involved (via their representatives) in management decision-making.

The aims of involvement may be:

(a) To generate commitment to the organisation

(b) To help the organisation improve performance, especially in the face of change

(c) To enable the organisation to better meet changing customer requirements

(d) To improve the challenge and satisfaction of the work experience

(e) To aid the organisation in attracting and retaining skilled labour

(f) To develop the business awareness of labour at all levels

(g) To increase employee incentives and accountabilities through tying reward to company performance and profitability, and/or

(h) To marginalise trade unions.

Guest (2001) describes five ways to get employees involved.

- By improving the provision of information to employees
- By improving the provision of information from employees
- By changing the structure and arrangement of work
- By changing the incentives
- By changing relationships, through more participative leadership and informality.

Activity 6 **(15 minutes)**

Suggest three techniques (already encountered in this Course Book) by which each of the above could be implemented.

Marchington *et al* (1992) similarly divide employee involvement schemes into four categories.

(a) **Downwards communications:** from managers to other employees and so on. This includes house journals, employee reports and briefings.

(b) **Upwards problem-solving forms:** designed to tap into individual and team knowledge and expertise. This includes suggestion schemes, attitude surveys, quality circles, customer care programmes and so on.

(c) **Financial participation:** linking rewards of individuals to the performance of the unit or business. This includes profit sharing, employee share ownership and factory-wide or value added bonus schemes (discussed in Chapter 5).

(d) **Representative participation:** employees are involved in decision-making through their representatives on JCCs, advisory councils, works councils, or collective bargaining. (This may operate at different levels of involvement, from consultation and dialogue to co-determination and even to control, eg in worker-managed teams or co-operatives.)

In addition, involvement may be encouraged by:

(a) **Empowerment**: the devolving of control and responsibility to individuals or teams at the workplace or 'front line' customer-service level. Empowerment may be 'soft' (providing enhanced opportunities for involvement in decision-making, fewer status barriers, more open communication, greater flexibility) or 'hard' (devolution of responsibility and accountability: standards and targets, monitoring and control)

(b) **Inclusion in the cultural and strategic priorities of the business.** Employees are invited and encouraged to share in commitment to quality, customer care, continuous improvement, learning and so on. This is frequently linked to empowerment as a set of guiding values and objectives within which teams can be more or less self-managing.

We will now look at some of these techniques in more detail.

4.2 Downward communication

Downward communication is usually well established in an organisation in the form of instructions, job briefings, rules and policies and announcement of plans by managers to staff.

There may, however, be potential for more empowering downward information flow about a wider range of matters, including: company strategy and future plans; positive performance feedback, celebrating individual, team and company achievements; competitor and other environmental factors that may influence work (or stimulating problem-solving); and so on.

Examples of mechanisms for downward communication of this type (see also Figure 6.2, earlier) include:

(a) **In-house journals,** bulletins and newsheets (and their electronic equivalents by e-mail or intranet pages). This is commonly used to foster a sense of involvement and belonging, but may be made a tool for greater participation by including various mechanisms for feedback and interaction: suggestion schemes, 'letter' pages, discussion forums, noticeboards and so on.

(b) **Team briefings,** where management pass information face-to-face to team members, on a regular basis. This enables people to feel that they know what is going on, and have access to the information required to do their work. Briefing meetings can also be used for interactive question-and-answer and problem-solving, however, for a more participative element.

(c) **Management by Walking Around**. The managerial culture of some organisations will need to be changed in order to increase information flow to employees. The hoarding of information as a source of power by managers, or the withholding of information on a 'need to know' basis are a feature of command-and-control cultures rather than facilitate-and-empower organisations.

FOR DISCUSSION

Is there too much information flowing around organisations – or does keeping employees 'in the loop' meaningfully contribute to employee relations?

4.3 Upward communication

Upward communication is rarer than downward – but vital to many modern organisations in:

(a) Providing feedback on progress and performance, so that plans can be adjusted where necessary

(b) Harnessing the experience and know-how of employees for innovation, problem-solving and decision-making

(c) Giving management insight into employees' needs, interests and problems, to help them manage better

(d) Demonstrating the value management places on employees, establishing the mutual trust and commitment that underpins constructive employee relations.

Mechanisms for upward communication include the following.

Attitude surveys

Surveys of employee opinions are a useful source of feedback (especially if there are no other direct avenues for employees to express their satisfactions and dissatisfactions). Attitude surveys may be carried out via:

(a) **Questionnaires**, whether standardised or tailored to the particular organisation or issue concerned. These may be paper-based or (increasingly) posted online on a company intranet. Questionnaires have the advantage of being quick and relatively cost-effective to administer, although they must be carefully designed if they are to elicit honest, meaningful and comparable responses.

(b) **Interviews**, either completely free-flowing or structured to a specific agenda of issues. Interviews are time-consuming and costly, but may also be more revealing, allowing a skilled interviewer to probe.

(c) **Focus groups**, allowing a structured response to interview questions by a representative sample of employees on specific issues

The CIPD has produced the following checklist for conducting an employee attitude survey.

(a) Gain the commitment of senior management, clarify objectives and define areas where the company is prepared to take action.

(b) Decide between a census of employees – probably paper-based – and a random sample – maybe face-to-face interviews.

(c) Conduct a pilot survey.

(d) Design a questionnaire – this needs experienced help.

(e) Tell employees what is being done: the more internal publicity, the greater the chances of success.

(f) Guarantee confidentiality.

(g) Consider measures to improve the response rate, for example by holding supervised completion sessions in company time.

(h) If the survey involves face-to-face interviews, conduct them with one or two employees at a time. Avoid group discussions – it is difficult to maintain confidentiality in groups and to enable everyone to have a say.

(i) Produce the final report. Distil the evidence, reach conclusions and put forward recommendations. Present the report to top management.

(j) Report back to employees with a summary of the main findings.

(k) An individual or a group should be made responsible for action following the survey findings; progress should be monitored.

Activity 7 **(15 minutes)**

How would you respond to the following objections from a management traditionalist to employee surveys?

(a) Good managers already know their staff's opinions.

(b) Surveys are superficial, impersonal and bureaucratic.

(c) Surveys open cans of worms and raise false hopes.

(d) Surveys contain built in bias because of the unknown opinions of the many who do not respond.

Suggestion schemes

Suggestion schemes are a way of offering performance rewards and incentives. They are also an important mechanisms for upward communication.

EXAMPLE

'What's the big idea, Vodafone?

'Vodafone is running a campaign to promote innovation: in the workforce. "My big idea" has already generated 500 ideas from employees aimed at improving customer experience, products and services.

'The ideas amassed so far will be whittled down to five with the finalists presenting their suggestions to the board later this month. The winning idea will be assessed for feasibility and rolled out next year.

'Dawn McIntyre, an HR business partner at Vodafone, told PM: "It's important to encourage staff to come up with ideas, and firms that don't do that are missing out as it's key to employee satisfaction."'

(*People Management*, 9 November 2006)

Quality circles

Definition

> **Quality circles** are groups of six to ten employees from different levels and/or disciplines within an organisation, who meet regularly to discuss problems of quality, quality control, customer care or related issues in their area of work.

Quality circles emerged first in the US but were most enthusiastically adopted in Japan. They are still used to get employees involved in organisational quality values, but some commentators suggest that they have been superseded by other team-based working methods and a wider orientation to quality in organisations (such as a Total Quality Management orientation).

The circle is facilitated by a leader who directs the discussion and helps to orient and develop members (as required) in quality control and problem-solving techniques. It is important that the group is made up of volunteers, in order to harness genuine commitment and enthusiasm.

Quality circles do not generally have responsibility for making, implementing or following up recommendations. Even as discussion groups, however, they may have significant benefits, as members return to their departments as ambassadors for quality, customer care and employee involvement.

FOR DISCUSSION

Why might values such as quality or customer care be a powerful focus for attempts to involve employees?

4.4 Empowerment

Empowerment has two key aspects. It involves giving workers discretion to make decisions about how to organise work in order to achieve task goals *and* making workers responsible for achieving production and quality targets. (The French word for empowerment is '*responsibilisation*'.)

The purpose of empowerment is:

(a) To free employees from rigorous control by instructions and orders, which contributes to job satisfaction *and* learning and flexibility

(b) To give employees opportunities for growth and job satisfaction through taking responsibility for their ideas and actions

(c) To release and develop resources in the workforce that would otherwise remain inaccessible, including creativity and initiative

(d) To harness employee commitment by allowing them to share in the process of target-setting and work organisation

(e) To decentralise decision-making and problem-solving initiative to 'front line' customer-facing roles, to enhance the flexibility and responsiveness of customer service.

Empowerment goes hand in hand with:

(a) **Delayering**, or a cut in the number of levels in the organisation hierarchy: responsibility previously held by managers is, in effect, being given to operational workers

(b) **Flexibility**, since giving responsibility to the people closest to the product or customer encourages responsiveness

(c) **New technology**, since skilled knowledge workers need less supervision, being better equipped to identify and control the means to clearly understood ends

(d) **Employee development**, since the personal and interpersonal skills needed to meet the challenges of responsibility and participation in decision-making need to be developed

(e) **Unitarist employee relations**, since empowerment rests on the belief that employees will recognise and commit themselves to the business goals of their unit and organisation.

Empowerment implies a shift in the role of both **line managers** (who effectively become 'coaches' and 'facilitators' in team decision-making processes, setting parameters and providing information and guidance where required) and **HR practitioners** (who increasingly share responsibility for delivering HR policy outcomes not only with line managers but with employees themselves).

EXAMPLE

The validity of this view and its relevance to modern trends appears to be borne out by the approach to empowerment adopted by **Harvester restaurants**, as described in *Personnel Management*. The management structure comprises a branch manager and a 'coach', while everyone else is a team member. Everyone within a team has one or more 'accountabilities' (these include recruitment, drawing up rotas, keeping track of sales targets and so on) which are shared out by the team members at their weekly team meetings. All the team members at different times act as 'co-ordinator' – the person responsible for taking the snap decisions that are frequently necessary in a busy restaurant. Apparently, all the staff involved agree that empowerment has made their jobs more interesting and had hugely increased their motivation and sense of involvement.

We will look briefly at two approaches to empowerment: self-managed teamworking and total quality management (TQM).

4.5 Self-managed teams

Self-managed teams are the most highly-developed form of team working. They are permanent structures in which team members collaboratively decide all the major issues affecting their work: work processes and schedules, task allocation, the selection and development of team members, the distribution of rewards and the management of group processes (problem-solving, conflict management, internal discipline and so on). The team leader is a member of the team, acting in the role of coach and facilitator: leadership roles may be shared or rotated as appropriate.

Self managed teams generally have the following features (Harrington-Mackin, 1994).

(a) They contract with management to assume various degrees of **managerial responsibility** for planning, organising, directing and monitoring (which may increase as the team develops). Team members learn and share the jobs usually performed by a manager: no 'visible' immediate manager is present. They often report to 'absentee' managers with broad responsibilities for several functions, whose role is to act as integrators/facilitators.

(b) They perform **day-to-day planning and control functions**: scheduling and co-ordinating the daily and occasional tasks of the team and individuals; setting performance goals and standards; formulating and adopting budgets; collecting performance data and reviewing results.

(c) They perform **internal people management functions**: screening and interviewing candidates to join the team, and contributing to selection/hiring decisions; providing orientation for new members; coaching and providing feedback on member performance; designing and conducting cross-training on all tasks.

(d) Team members **cross-train** in all the tasks necessary for a particular process, and members rotate flexibly from job to job.

(e) **Weekly team meetings** are used to identify, analyse and solve task and relationship problems within the team: reviewing team working and progress; getting team members to research and present team issues and so on.

Activity 8 **(20 minutes)**

What do you think are likely to be the advantages of self-managed teamworking for the organisation?

4.6 Total quality management (TQM)

TQM is a Japanese-inspired orientation to quality in which quality values and aspirations are applied to the management of *all* resources and relationships within the firm and throughout the value chain (from suppliers to distributors), in order to seek continuous improvement and excellence in all aspects of performance.

Mullins (1999) synthesises various definitions of TQM as expressing: 'a way of life for an organisation as an whole, committed to total customer satisfaction through a continuous process of improvement, and the contribution and involvement of people'.

Two key aspects of TQM are:

(a) **Quality chains**. The quality chain extends from suppliers through to customers, via the 'internal customers' of each department within the organisation. The chain may be broken at any point where people or processes fail to fulfil the quality requirements of their immediate customer.

(b) **Total involvement**. Quality requires the commitment of all staff, and needs to be modelled from the top by senior management. It needs to be supported and reinforced by HRM policies for recruitment, training, appraisal, reward and development. It also emphasises the importance of people: communication, awareness and problem-solving are more important than mere systems.

FOR DISCUSSION

On a scale from 'no voice' through involvement and participation to full empowerment or democracy, where would you place the orgnisation you currently work for, or one you know well?

Chapter roundup

- Employee voice embraces 'a whole variety of processes and structures which enable, and sometimes empower employees, directly and indirectly, to contribute to decision-making in the firm.
- Employee participation concerns the extent to which employees, often via their representatives, are involved with management in the decision-making machinery of the organisation. It includes joint consultation, works councils, European Works Councils and worker representation on the board.
- Employee involvement is the process of informing and consulting employees about, or associating them with, one or more aspects of running an organisation. It may be accomplished by two-way communication, financial participation, representative participation, empowerment and inclusion in cultural programmes such as quality management and organisational learning

Quick quiz

1 Distinguish between the terms 'employee voice', 'employee participation' and 'employee involvement'.

2 Draw Marchington *et al*'s matrix model of employee voice.

3 Give three examples of 'representative participation'.

4 What is joint consultation?

5 What is an EWC and when is it compulsory to have one?

6 A partnership agreement reflects a pluralist approach to employee relations. True or false?

7 Outline the German model of co-determination.

8 Give five examples of employee involvement techniques.

9 What are the purposes of empowerment?

10 What is TQM?

Answers to quick quiz

1 Employee voice covers the range of possibilities from no voice through to full participation. Involvement is consultation/communication where management retains the right to manage. Participation allows employees to influence organisational decisions. (para 1.1)

2 See Figure 6.1.

3 Collective representation, joint consultation, European Works Council, partnership agreements. (para 1.3)

4 Formal non-negotiatory meetings between management and employee representatives to discuss matters of shared interest. (para 2.3)

5 A Pan-European body of employee representatives with the right to meet central management at least once a year for information and consultation about the progress and prospects of the company. All organisations with more than 1,000 employees in the EU member states, with more than 150 people in each of two or more states, must establish some form of Europe-wide consultational system: an EWC is the fallback system if unions and employee negotiators fail to agree on an alternative. (para 2.4)

6 False: unitarist. (para 2.7)

7 See paragraph 3.3 for a full answer.

8 Communication (eg briefings, journals)

Up-down communication (eg suggestion schemes, quality circles)

Financial participation (eg profit-sharing, share ownership)

Representative participation (eg joint consultation, works councils)

Empowerment (eg self-managed teamworking, delegation)

Cultural programmes (eg TQM, customer care, learning organisation)
(**Note:** the activity only required five.) (para 4.1)

9 Total Quality Management: a whole-organisation approach to managing quality through the application of quality values, continuous improvement and total involvement. (para 4.6)

10 See paragraph 4.4 for a full answer.

Answers to activities

1 Participation may be desirable or necessary because of the following factors.

(a) **Commitment**: the perceived need to obtain a higher level of identification with organisational goals and a higher degree of acceptance and support of strategies for change.

(b) **Quality of decision-making**: the perceived need to involve employees with 'front-line' knowledge, experience and influence in areas such as quality management and customer care. Quality circles and empowered teams are developed on this basis.

(c) **Trade union pressure.** Collective bargaining has been extended into areas traditionally considered as management concerns: human resource levels, training and so on. Joint consultation is another prevalent form of worker participation, where management discuss matters of concern regularly with union representatives, on Joint Consultative Committees (JCCs) or non-negotiatory staff forums. A more radical approach is the formation of partnership agreements with worker representatives.

(d) **Legal requirements**. Participation and consultation have occupied a high profile in employment protection and – most recently – in the social policy of the European Union, with provision for employee representation in decision-sharing structures such as Works Councils and Supervisory Boards.

2 Your own research.

3 Your own research (and opinion).

4 Some advantages (identified by Legal & General and MSF in their partnership agreement) include:

(a) Increased flexibility, honesty and trust in relationships

(b) Better quality, faster decision-making, with decisions that were more likely to be readily accepted within the company

(c) Positive public relations for the company – and for the union ('rebranded' to attract new members)

(d) Having the right people focused on the right issues

(e) The development of an 'adult' relationship in which company and union could move in the same direction

5 Low power-distance and collectivist cultures are particularly likely to accept employee participation at a deep level.

6 (a) Briefing groups and meetings, Joint Consultation Committees or works councils, open direct communication from managers, encouraging informal networking, 360° feedback, consultation policy, noticeboards/memos etc.

(b) Suggestion schemes, quality circles, upward appraisal, JCCs or works councils, attitude surveys

(c) Increased delegation (empowerment), self-managed and/or multi-skilled teamworking, horizontal structures focused on the customer, job design based on whole meaningful tasks

(d) Financial participation through profit-related pay, employee share ownership schemes; cafeteria benefits; learning/development opportunities

(e) Participative management style; single status agreements; culture of informality (Management By Walking Around); role of supervisor as coach/facilitator.

7 Nigel Nicholson (*Financial Times*, January 1993) gave the following answers (briefly summarised).

(a) How do managers know if their reading of opinions is correct?

(b) Yes, they are no substitute for good personal communications, but 'Thanks for asking us' is a common response.

(c) Cans of worms probably should be opened. 'Management's commitment, clearly communicated at the outset, should be not only to take action where feasible, but also to be frank about reasons for not acting when this would be unreasonably difficult, contentious or costly.

(d) Bias is modest when return rates of over 50% are achieved, and a well-designed and carefully introduced survey can expect returns of 65% or more.

8 Self-managed teamworking is said to have advantages in:

- Savings in managerial costs
- Gains in quality and productivity, by harnessing the commitment of those who perform work
- Encouraging individual initiative and responsibility, enhancing organisational responsiveness (particularly in front-line customer service units)
- Gains in efficiency, through multi-skilling, the involvement of fewer functions in decision-making and co-ordinating work, and (often) the streamlining of working methods by groups

However, self-managed teams are a comparatively recent (and rare) phenomenon, and require skilled leadership and culture change (particularly in former 'command and control' organisations) in order to be effective.

Bibliography

Adair, J & Allen, M (1999) *Time Management and Personal Development*. London: Hawksmere

Adams, J S (1963), 'Toward an understanding of inequity' *Journal of Abnormal & Social Psychology* 64/4.

Alberga, T, Tyson, S & Parsons, D (1997) 'An evaluation of the Investors in People Standard', *Human Resource Management Journal* 7 (2)

Albrecht, K & Albrecht, S (1993) 'Added Value Negotiating', *Training*, April pp 26-29

Armstrong, M (2000) *Strategic Human Resource Management: A Guide to Action* (2nd edition). London: Kogan Page

Allen, A (2003) 'Out of the ordinary', *People Management*, 4 December

Armstrong, M (2003) *A Handbook of Human Resource Management Practice* (9th edition). London: Kogan Page

Arnold, J, Copper, C & Robertson, I (1995) *Work Psychology: Understanding Human Behaviour in the Workplace* (2nd edition). London: Pitman

Atkinson, J (1984) 'Manpower strategies for flexible organisations' *Personnel Management*, August

Atkinson, J & Meager, N (1986) *Changing patterns of Work*. London: IMS/OECD

Barnes, P (1997) 'Teleworking'. *Chartered Secretary*, May

Beardwell, I & Holden, L (1997) *Human Resource Management* (2nd edition). London: Pitman

Beer, M, Spector B, Laurence P, Quinn Mills, D & Walton, K (1984) *Managing Human Assets*. New York: Free Press

Beer, M & Spector, B (1985) 'Corporate transformations in human resource management', *HRM Trends and Challenges* (ed Walton & Lawrence). Boston, Mass: Harvard University Press

Blyth, A (2003) 'The art of survival', *People Management*, 1 May

Blyton, P & Turnbull, P (1992) *Reassessing HRM*. London: Sage

Bolton, T (1997) *Human Resource Management: An Introduction*. Oxford: Blackwell

Bond, S (2003) 'How to effect changes in working hours', *People Management*, 10 July

Bottomley, C (1998) in *People Management*, 9 September

Boxall, P F (1995) 'Building the theory of comparative HRM', *HRM Journal*, 5 (5)

Boxall, P F & Purcell, J (2003) *Strategy and Human Resource Management*. Basingstoke: Palgrave Macmillan

Bramley, P (1986) *Evaluation of Training: A practical guide*. London: BASIE

Bratton, J & Gold, J (2007) *Human Resource Management: Theory and Practice* (4th edition). Basingstoke: Palgrave Macmillan

Brewster, C (1999) 'Strategic HRM: the value of different paradigms', *Strategic Human Resource Management* (ed Schuler, Jackson). Oxford: Blackwell

Bridges, W (1994) *Jobshift: How to Prosper in a Workplace Without Jobs*. London: Allen & Unwin

Bronstein, M (2003), 'A life less ordinary', *People Management*, 17 April

Brown, D & Baron, A (2003) 'A capital idea' *People Management*, 26 June

Budhwar, P S and Mellahi (2006) *Managing Human Resources in the Middle East.* Abingdon, Oxon: Routledge

Burgoyne, J (1999) *Developing Yourself, Your Career and Your Organisation.* London: Lemos & Crane

Burns, J M (1978) *Leadership.* London: Harper & Row

Cartright, A (2003) 'How to deal with requests for flexible working', *People Management*, 6 November

Chamberlain, N W & Kuhn, J (1965) *Collective Bargaining.* New York: McGraw Hill

CIPD (1994) *Statement on Counselling in the Workplace.* London: CIPD

Clague, I (2004) 'Soft touch strategies', posted at www.learningtechnologies.co/article on 02/03/04

Clarke, K (2003) 'Show me the money' *People Management*, 1 May

Clegg, H (1976) *The System of Industrial Relations in Great Britain.* Oxford: Blackwell

Clutterbuck, D (1991) *Everyone Needs a Mentor: How to Foster Talent Within the Organisation* (2nd edition). London: IPM

Connock, S (1991) *HR Vision: Managing a Quality Workforce.* London: IPM

Constable, R & McCormick, R J (1987) *The Making of British Managers.* London: BIM

Cooper, C (2003) 'Minority report', *People Management*, 4 December

Cornelius & Faire, S (1989) *Everyone Can Win: How to Resolve Conflict.* Sydney: Simon & Schuster Australia

Critchley, R (1996). 'New paradigms for "sustainable employability"', *HR Monthly*, April, pp 22-23

Cuming, M W (1993) *The Theory and Practice of Personnel Management.* London: Butterworth Heinemann

Cushway, B & Lodge, D (1994) *Human Resource Management.* Nichols

Dalgamo, D & Davies, P (2003) 'How to consult on collective redundancies', *People Management*, 11 September

Department for Education and Employment (1998) *The Learning Age: a renaissance for a new Britain.* Sheffield: DfEE

Department for Education and Employment (1999) *Learning to Succeed: a new framework for post-16 education.* Sheffield: DfEE

Department for Education and Employment (2000) *Labour Market and Skill Trends.* Sheffield: DfEE

Dobler, D W, Burt D N & Lee, L (1990) *Purchasing and Materials Management.* (5th edition) New York: McGraw Hill

Drucker, P (1955). *The Practice of Management.* London: Heinemann

Equal Opportunities Commission (2000) *Good Practice Guide: Job evaluation schemes free of sex bias*. Manchester: EOC

Evans, J (2003) 'DTI official hints at tougher law', *People Management*, 10 July

Fisher, R, Ury, W & Patton, B (1999) *Getting to Yes: Negotiating an Agreement Without Giving In* (2nd edition). London: Random House

Fombrun, C J, Tichy, N M & Devanno, M A (1984) *Strategic Human Resource Management*. New York: Wiley

Fox, A (1975) *Industrial Relations and a Wider Society: Aspects of Interaction*. London: Faber & Faber

Gardenswartz, L & Rowe, A (1993) *Managing Diversity: A Complete Desk Reference and Planning Guide*. Homewood, IL: Irwin

Garvin, M (1993) 'Building a Learning Organisation', *Harvard Business Review*, July-August

Gennard, J and Judge, G *Employee Relations* (3rd edition). London: CIPD

Goldthorpe, J H, Lockwood, D C, Bechofer, F & Platt, J (1968) *The Affluent Worker: Industrial Attitudes and Behaviour*. Cambridge: CUP

Goleman, D C (1998) Working with Emotional Intelligence. London: Bloomsbury

Goss, D (1994) *Principles of Human Resource Management*. London: International Thomson Business Press

Graham, H T & Bennett, R (1998) *Human Resources Management* (9th edition). London: Pitman

Gratton, L, Haily, V H, Stile, P & Truss, C (1999) *Strategic HRM*. Oxford: OUP

Guest, D E (1989) 'Personnel & HRM: Can you tell the difference?' *Personnel Management*, January pp 48-51

Guest, D E (1991) 'Personnel management: the end of orthodoxy', *British Journal of Industrial Relations* 29 (2)

Guest, D E (1999) 'Human Resource Management: the workers' verdict', *Human Resource Management Journal* 9 (2)

Guest, D E (2001) 'Industrial relations and HRM', *Human Resource Management: A Critical Text* (2nd edition) (ed Storey). London: Thomson

Guest, D E, Michie, J, Sheehan, M & Conway, N (2000) *Employment Relations, HRM & Business Performance*. London: CIPD

Guirdham, M (1999) *Communicating Across Cultures*. Basingstoke: Palgrave

Handy, C B (1989) *The Age of Unreason*. London: Business Books

Handy, C B (1993) *Understanding Organisations*. Harmondsworth: Penguin

Hargreaves, P & Jarvis, P (2000) *The Human Resource Development Handbook* (revised edition). London: Kogan Page

Hersey, P & Blanchard, K H (1988) *Management of Organisational Behaviour: Utilising Human Resources* (5th edition). New Jersey: Prentice Hall

Herzberg, F W (1966) *Work and the Nature of Man*. New York: Staples

Higginbottom, K (2003 (a)) 'More than lip service' *People Management*, 4 December

Higginbottom, K (2003 (b)) 'HR in the spotlight' *People Management*, 20 November

Higginbottom, K (2003 (c)) 'Mind your own business', *People Management*, 1 May

Hofstede, G (1989) *Cultures Consequences*. Beverley Hills, CA: Sage

Hofstede, G (1991) *Cultures and Organisations*. London: McGraw Hill

Holmstrom, R (2003) 'Time well spent', *People Management*, 28 August

Honey, P & Mumford, A (1990) *The Opportunist Learner*. Maidenhead: Peter Honey

Honey, P & Mumford, A (1992) *A Manual of Learning Styles* (3rd edition). Maidenhead: Peter Honey

Huczynski, A & Buchanan, D (2001) *Organisational Behaviour: An Introductory Text*. Harlow, Essex: FT Prentice Hall

Hunt, J (1982) *Managing People in Organisations*. NY: McGraw Hill

Huthwaite Inc (2000) *Behaviour of Successful Negotiators*. Percellville, VI: Huthwaite Inc.

Ingham, J (2003) 'How to implement a diversity policy', *People Management*, 24 July

Investors in People (2004) posted at www.investorsinpeople.co.uk/IIP/...CaseStudies, 12.02.04

IPD (1998) *The IPD Guide to Outsourcing*. London: IPD

IPM (1992) *Statement on Counselling in the Workplace*. London: IPM

Ivey, A, Ivey, M & Simek Morgan, L (1993) *Counselling and Psychotherapy: a Multicultural Perspective* (3rd edition). Boston, Mass: Allyn & Bacon

Johns, E (1994) *Perfect Customer Care*. London: Random House

Jones, B (1982) *Sleepers, Wake!: Technology and the Future of Work*. Oxford: OUP

Kane & Stanton (1994) *Human Resource Planning in a Changing Environment.*

Katz, R (ed) *Career Issues in Human Resource Management*. New Jersey: Prentice Hall

Kaufman, R & Keller, J M (1994) 'Levels of Evaluation: Beyond Kirkpatrick', *HRP Quarterly* (5)

Kirkpatrick, D L (1998) *Evaluating Training Programmes: the Four Levels*. San Francisco: Berrett-Koehler

Kohn, A (1993) 'Why incentive plans cannot work', *Harvard Business Review*, Sep-Oct pp 54-63

Kolb, D (1984) *Experiential Learning*. New York: Prentice Hall

Kramar, R, McGraw, P & Schuler, R (1997), *Human Resource Management in Australia* (3rd edition). Melbourne: Addison Wesley Longman

Leat, M (2007) Exploring Employee Relations (2nd edition) Oxford: Butterworth-Heinemann

Legge, K (1989) 'Human Resource Management: a critical analysis', *New Perspectives in HRM* (ed Storey). London: Routledge

Legge, K (1998) 'The morality of HRM', *Experiencing HRM* (ed Mabey, Skinner & Clark). Cambridge

Liff, S (2000) 'Manpower or HR planning: what's in a name?' *Personnel Management* (3rd edition) eds Bach & Sisson. Oxford: Blackwell

Livy, B (1988) *Corporate Personnel Management.* London: Pitman

Lockett, J (1992) *Effective Performance Management.* Kogan Page

LSC (2004 (a)), posted at www.lsc.gov.uk/National/media/News/Nationalemployersurvey on 02/02/04

LSC (2004 (b)), posted at www.lsc.gov.uk/National/media/PressReleases/ASDAMA on 18.02.04

Lupton, T (1974) *Wages and Salaries*. London: Penguin

Maier, N (1958) *The Appraisal Interview*. New York: Wiley

Manocha, R (2003) 'Catch 22', *People Management*, 9 October

Marchington, M, Goodman, J, Wilkinson, A & Ackers, P (1992) *New Developments in Employee Involvement*. London: HMSO

Marchington, M, Wilkinson, A, Ackers, P & Dundon, A (2001) *Management Choice and Employee Voice*. London: CIPD

Margolis, A (2003) 'Licenced to skill', *People Management*, 26 June

Martin, A O (1967) *Welfare at Work*. London: Batsford

Maslow, A (1954) *Motivation and Personality*. New York: Harper & Row

McGregor, D (1987) *The Human Side of Enterprise*. London: Penguin

Mowdray, R, Porter, L & Steers, R (1982) *Employee-Organisation Linkages* London: Academic Press

Moxon, G R (1958) *Functions of a Personnel Department.* London: IPM

Mullins, L (1985) 'The personnel function: a shared responsibility' *The Administrator*, May

Mullins, L (1999) *Management and Organisational Behaviour* (5th edition). Harlow, Essex: FT Prentice Hall

Mumford, A (1994) *Management Development: Strategies for Action*. London: IPM

Munro Fraser, J (1971) *Psychology: General, Industrial, Social*. London: Pitman

National Skills Task Force (1998) *Towards a National Skills Agenda.* London: DfEE

National Skills Task Force (2000) *Skills for All: research report from the NSTK.* London: DfEE

Ouchi, W (1981) *Theory Z*. Reading, Mass: Addison Wesley

Overman, S (2003) 'HR drives change at Levis', *People Management*, 6 November

Oxford Institute of International Finance (2002) *Managing Self Development.* London: OITF

Parsloe, E & Wray, M (2000) *Coaching and Mentoring: Practical Methods to Improve Learning*. London: Kogan Page

Pedler, M Burgoyne, J & Boydell, T (1991) *The Learning Company*. Maidenhead: McGraw Hill

Pedler, M, Burgoyne, J & Boydell, T (2001) *A Manager's Guide to Self Development* (4th edition) Maidenhead: McGraw Hill

Pedler, M, Brook, C & Burgoyne, J (2003) 'Motion Pictures', *People Management*, 17 April

Persaud, J (2003) 'Fitness First', *People Management*, 11 September

Personnel Standards Lead Body (1993) *A Perspective on Personnel*. London: PSLB

Peters, T J & Waterman, R (1982) *In Search of Excellence*. New York: Harper & Row

Peters, T J (1989) *Thriving on Chaos*. New York: Pan

Peters, T J (1994) *Liberation Management*. New York: Pan

Phillips, J (1997) *Return on Investment in Training and Performance Improvement Programs*. Houston, TX: Gulf

Pickard, J (2003) 'Joint effort', *People Management*, 24 July

Plumbley, P (1991) *Recruitment and Selection* (5th edition). Hyperion

Prasad, R (2003) Connexions Special Supplement, *The Guardian*, January 29

Purcell, J, Kinnie, N & Hutchinson, S (2003) 'Inside the black box' *People Management*, 15 May

Ream, B (1984) *Personnel Administration*. London: ICSA

Rees, W D (1996) *The Skills of Management* (4th edition). London: Thomson Business Press

Roberts, Z (2003 (a)) 'Barclays banks on older staff', *People Management*, 29 May

Roberts, Z (2003 (b)) 'BT drive for top women', *People Management*, 11 September

Roberts, Z (2003 (c)) 'Fast-track learning', *People Management*, 10 July

Rodger, A (1970) *The Seven Point Plan* (3rd edition) London: NFER

Rosenberg, M (2003) 'Best laid plans', *People Management*, 3 April

Schein, E H (1985) *Organisational Culture and Leadership*. San Francisco: Jossey Bass

Schneider, S & Barsoux, J (1997) *Managing Across Cultures*. Harlow, Essex: FT Prentice Hall

Schuler, R S (1995) *Managing Human Resources*. St Paul, Minn: West Publishing

Senge, P (1990) *The Fifth Discipline: the Art and Practice of the Learning Organisation.* New York: Random Century

Shepherd, C (2004) 'Assessing the ROI of training', www.fastrak-consulting.co.uk/tactix/features on 02/03/2004

Sisson, K & Storey, J (2000) *The Realities of HRM: Managing the employment relationship.* Buckingham: OUP

Sloman, M (2001) *The e-Learning Revolution*. London: CIPD

Sloman, M (2003) 'Learning Curve', *People Management,* 25 September

Solomon, C M (2001) 'Managing Virtual Teams', *Workforce*, June

Stone, F M (1999) *Coaching, Counselling and Mentoring.* New York: AMACOM

Storey, J (1989) 'From personnel management to human resource management', *New Perspective on HRM* (ed Storey). London: Routledge

Storey, J (1992) *New Developments in the Management of Human Resources*. London: Routledge

Taylor, S (1998) *Employee Resourcing*. London: IPD

Torrington, D (1994) *International Personnel Management*. Englewood Cliffs, NJ: Prentice Hall

Torrington, D & Hall, L (1991) *Personnel Management: A New Approach*. Englewood Cliffs, NJ: Prentice Hall

Torrington, D, Hall, L, Taylor, S (2002) *Human Resource Management* (5th edition). London: Pearson Education

Townsend, R (1985) *Further up the organisation*. London: Hodder & Stoughton

Trades Union Congress (2000) *Qualifying for Racism*. London: TUC

Trompenaars, F (1993) *Riding the Waves of Culture*. London: Nicholas Brealey

Tulip, S (2003 (a)) 'Just rewards', *People Management*, 25 September

Tyson S (2006) *Essentials of Human Resource Management* (5th Edition) Oxford: Butterworth-Heinemann

Tyson, S & Fell, A (1986) *Evaluating the Personnel Function.* London: Hutchinson

University for Industry (2003) 'UfI/learndirect well placed to deliver Government's e-learning vision', posted at www.ufi.com/press/releases on 08/07/03

Upton, R (2003) 'Star gazers', *People Management*, 26 June

Vroom, V (1964) *Work and motivation*. New York: Wiley

Walsh, M (2004) 'Ill winds offshore', *The Bulletin*, February 3

Watkins, J (2003 (a)) 'Staff turnover hits four-year low', *People Management*, 4 December

Watkins, J (2003 (b)) 'Tests cut EA turnover', *People Management*, 25 September

Watkins, J (2003 (c)) 'Stress busters', *People Management*, 25 September

Watkins, J (2003 (d)) 'Serious turbulence', *People Management*, 7 August

Watkins, J & Staines, K (2003) 'Job firm risks discrimination', *People Management*, 15 May

Welch, J (2003) 'In the hiring line', *People Management*, 26 June

Whetten, D, & Cameron, K (2002) *Developing Management Skills* (5th edition). New Jersey: Prentice Hall

Whetten, D, Cameron, K & Woods, M (2000) *Developing Management Skills for Europe* (2nd edition). Harlow, Essex: FT Prentice Hall

Wild, A (2003) 'Pressure point', *People Management*, 10 July

Wood, R and Payne, T (1998) *Competency-based Recruitment and Selection.* Chichester: Wiley

Woodruffe, C (1992) 'What is meant by a competency?' *Designing and Achieving Competency* (ed Boam & Sparrow). Maidenhead: McGraw Hill

Woolnough, R (2003) 'Child benefits', *People Management*, 4 December

Glossary

Collective bargaining is the process whereby employers and employee representatives negotiate agreements by which terms and conditions of employment (and related matters) are determined for groups of represented employees.

Competence may be defined as the skill, knowledge and behaviours that need to be applied for effective performance in a work context.

Development is the growth of people's knowledge and capabilities and the increasing fulfilment of their potential, through a range of learning experiences.

E-learning is: 'Learning that is delivered, enabled or mediated by electronic technology for the explicit purposes of training in organisations. It does not include stand-alone technology-based training such as the use of CD-ROMs in isolation.' (CIPD)

Employability describes a portfolio of knowledge, skills, competences and attributes that enhances an individual's mobility and power in the labour market. Employability training aims to equip employees with such a portfolio.

Employee involvement describes a wide range of policies and techniques for 'informing and consulting employees about, or associating them with, one or more aspects of running an organisation.'

Employee participation 'concerns the extent to which employees, often via their representatives, are involved in the decision-making machinery of the organisation. This includes joint consultation, collective bargaining and worker representation on the board' (Gennard & Judge, 2003).

Employee relations 'consist of all those areas of HRM that involve general relationships with employees, through collective agreements where trade unions are recognised [industrial relations] and/or through commonly applied policies for employee involvement and communications' (Armstrong, 2000).

An **independent trade union** is one which has been certified as being autonomous and financially self-supporting: not dominated by an employer because of the provision or withdrawal of financial or other support.

Industrial relations (IR) comprises 'all the rules, practices and conventions governing interactions between managements and their workforces, normally involving collective employee representation and bargaining.'

Joint consultation is a process by which management and employee representatives jointly examine and discuss issues of mutual concern.

Learning is the process whereby people acquire knowledge, capabilities and skills.

A **learning curve** is a graph showing the relationship between the time spent in learning and the level of competence attained. Hence, it describes the progress and variable pace of learning. (It is common for people to say that they are 'on a steep learning curve' when they have to acquire a lot of new knowledge or skills in a short period of time.)

A **learning organisation** is one that facilitates the acquisition and sharing of knowledge, and the learning of all its members, in order continuously and strategically to transform itself in response to a rapidly changing and uncertain environment, and to develop and refine the capabilities required for future success.

Management development is 'an attempt to improve managerial effectiveness through a planned and deliberate learning process'.

A **mentor** is a guide, ideally both more experienced and more powerful in the organisation, whose concern is the trainee's long-term personal development. The role is varied: counsellor, role model, champion/sponsor, spur to action or improvement, critical friend, encourager and so on.

Negotiation is a process whereby two parties come together to confer with a view to concluding a jointly acceptable agreement.

Partnership agreements are negotiated arrangements 'in which both parties (management and the trade union) agree to work together to their mutual advantage and to achieve a climate of more co-operative and therefore less adversarial industrial relations.'

Pendulum arbitration is a system whereby a third party will arbitrate on behalf of the two principals in collective bargaining, should they fail to reach agreement, by awarding the final position of one side or the other: either the employer's final offer or the employees' final claim.

Personal development plans (PDPs) are action plans for individuals' skill and career development which put the onus on the individuals themselves to seek out and organise training and development opportunities.

Quality circles are groups of six to ten employees from different levels and/or disciplines within an organisation, who meet regularly to discuss problems of quality, quality control, customer care or related issues in their area of work.

'**Return on investment** (ROI) is a measure of the monetary benefits obtained by an organisation over a specified time period in return for a given investment in a training programme. Looking at it another way, ROI is the extent to which the benefits (outputs) of training exceed the costs (inputs).' (Shepherd, 2004)

Single-table bargaining describes a situation in which the terms and conditions of all represented workers employed by an establishment are determined in a single set of negotiations. This could involve a single union representing different types and grades of employees (manual and non-manual), or several unions which negotiate a bargaining position amongst themselves prior to negotiating with management as a single bargaining unit.

Skill may be defined as a learned pattern of operations, or responses to stimuli, which allow the successful, rapid and apparently confident performance of a complex task.

Strike action is the withholding of labour in the course of a dispute with management.

A **trade union** is an organised association of employees who 'consist wholly or mainly of workers of one or more description and whose principal purposes include the regulation of relations between workers and employers' *(Trade Unions and Labour Relations (Consolidation) Act).*

Training is the use of planned, systematic instruction and other learning events and programmes to promote learning, with the particular aim of enhancing competence in a work role.

According to the Department of Employment, **training** is 'the systematic development of the attitude/knowledge/skill/behaviour pattern required by an individual in order to perform adequately a given task or job.'

Training needs may be defined as the gap between what people should be achieving and what they actually are achieving. In other words:

Required level of competence *minus* present level of competence = training need.

Transfer of learning refers to the extent to which newly learned information or skills have been transferred from the learning context to the application of a specific task.

Index